To Professor James Franck

with respect and admiration

H. Uri

BRITISH ART SINCE 1900

AN ANTHOLOGY BY
SIR JOHN ROTHENSTEIN

WITH 155 ILLUSTRATIONS

PHAIDON PRESS · LONDON

© 1962 PHAIDON PRESS LTD · LONDON SW7

MADE IN GREAT BRITAIN

TEXT AND COLOUR PLATES PRINTED BY HUNT, BARNARD AND CO LTD · AYLESBURY

PHOTOGRAVURE PLATES PRINTED BY VANDYCK PRINTERS LTD · BRISTOL

FOR HENRY MOORE

BRITISH ART SINCE 1900

THERE exists, so far as I am aware, no picture-book of British art of the present century. By way of introduction to this, the first of its kind, I propose to offer a few reflections about the activities and environment of painters, sculptors and draughtsmen in this country since 1900. These reflections are offered with diffidence, first because the judgement of contemporaries, as Henry James noted, is 'the most difficult of all forms of criticism'; second because there is today a degree of critical confusion without precedent. Hemmed in by the trees, the contemporary critic has but an imperfect notion of the wood's character – but perhaps jungle would be a more accurate description of those places where the arts are made, evaluated and sold. His efforts at perspective are frustrated by an imprecise idea of his own location in the wood, and his attempts to do justice by his inability to gauge the effects of his own prejudices and of the insidious pressures of fashion. But these are difficulties which beset all critics of contemporary activities at all times. The critic of today, however, has a unique difficulty to contend with. In all earlier periods there existed certain clearly recognized traditions which exercised a wide authority, and which were clearly recognized even at times when, as was generally the case, they were in transition. These traditions provided standards whereby the new things might be evaluated. The ideas of Ingres were not so remote from those of Delacroix or Courbet as to preclude closely reasoned debate, and even a measure of agreement. In the aesthetic of Delacroix, for example, classical ideas played a crucial part. But today traditional standards of any kind, far from being accepted as standards whereby the new thing may be judged, are deeply suspect, or else rejected outright. In brief, the historic respect for tradition is today replaced by its opposite: extreme mistrust, and a corresponding disposition to put faith in the new and the untraditional simply as the new and the untraditional. This 'demon of progress', as Wyndham Lewis called it, is not of course confined to the arts. Faith in the inevitability of progress – in the continuous replacement of the new by the different and the better – is an integral part of the prevailing pattern of thought with regard to many, perhaps most, spheres of human activity. That it should be held to be valid in relation to the fine arts might on first consideration strike us as singular, for it is contradicted with overwhelming authority by the facts of history. Lord Macaulay, one of the most optimistic of historians, advanced – in his essay on Milton – the view that 'as civilization advances, poetry almost necessarily declines', that it is in a rude state of society 'that we expect to find the poetical temperament in its highest perfection' and that 'the most wonderful and splendid proof of genius is a great poem produced in a civilized age'. Macaulay's contention, which he applies to music, painting and sculpture, as well as to poetry, is difficult to refute, and a glance through any general history of art will be sufficient to show that the arts do not progress. How then does it come about that there is today a widespread conviction to the contrary – a conviction by no means confined to the unthinking? It springs mainly from the circumstance that during the past century a galaxy of audaciously innovating masters appeared who were consistently held up to ridicule and abuse or else ignored, and the patronage and the honours with insignificant exceptions were reserved for those whose names and works are long forgotten. Daumier and Millet lived in poverty; Degas and Cézanne had, or came to have, other means of support than the practice of their art; Pissarro could barely maintain his family; Van Gogh was

I

spared from starvation by the charity of a penurious brother; Gauguin did starve and the Douanier Rousseau was dismissed as a joke. A few decades have sufficed to vindicate these men, to see them numbered among the masters, and to show the great majority – the public, the great collectors and the critics – to have been ludicrously wrong, and wrong, moreover, through taking their stand on 'tradition'. The resulting shock has unnerved public, collectors and critics, who, determined not to be caught again in the same undignified posture, now need little inducement to admire new works in inverse ratio to their resemblance to any already existing. Faced, for instance, with Action painting and *tachisme*, they remember all those Cézannes lying abandoned in garden and field, all those Van Goghs to be had for the price of a meal, and they raise a nervous cheer. (I intend at this point no reflection upon either of these revolutionary modes of painting, but merely to suggest that much of the awe, indeed the acclamation, with which they are received is due less to conviction than, quite simply, to loss of nerve.) The progressive change in the prevailing attitude towards innovation which has come about during the last hundred years is now complete: unthinking resistance to the new has become transformed into no less unthinking acceptance. So intimidating is this new disposition that moral courage is required to reject it and still more to treat it with levity, however ludicrous it be. Not that, even now, unqualified enthusiasm is felt to be without its dangers: innovation follows innovation with such rapidity that too wholehearted an acceptance of any particular one is liable to involve logical absurdities, and in any case each in turn is promptly and manifestly superseded. The safer course therefore is rather to recognize the principle of 'progress', but to allow for occasional aberration. Such, roughly speaking, is the attitude of the average person interested in the arts, the grandchild of the generation which was hostile, in so far as it was aware of them, to the impressionists and to Cézanne, Van Gogh, Gauguin and Seurat.

The critical confusion which prevails today is deepened by the measure of dominance still exercised by Paris. If Paris remained the almost unchallenged creative centre, or else the repository of some kind of central tradition, it might still give coherence to what now appears to be a prospect of almost absolute confusion. But it is no longer a capital legislating for provinces; no longer a focus of creativity unique in its originality, in its energy, in its variety, and accordingly in its authority, it continues nevertheless to occupy a unique position in the world of art. Some of the causes of its retention of something of its hold upon the art world are obvious enough: its beauty and amenity, and the treasures of the Louvre and its dependencies, make it art's fitting capital; it is a place where the visual arts are of deeper concern to more people than anywhere else; for those who care for the visual arts it is holy ground, as the house and the school of the masters, the home, even today, of Braque, and from time to time of Picasso. But there are other, less obvious causes. Great commercial interests are concerned to maintain the ascendancy of Paris, and one of the means they employ is to foster the notion that Paris is the breeding-ground and the shop-window of the latest innovation. The only innovations of value, however, are those which originate with men of serious talent, and the truth is that Paris today is short of serious talent. But the show must go on, and if there is not enough serious talent, then mere talent and mere taste and sometimes even effrontery must serve. That there flourish in Paris artists of rare gifts needs hardly be said. Giacometti, to give one outstanding instance, is happily at the height of his powers, but such artists are hopelessly inadequate to the mass requirements of the great commercial machine. In the relative paucity of serious talent, this machine mostly supplies modish novelties. Paris is therefore lending the magic of its prestige neither to original creation nor to a tradition but predominantly to fostering the heresy of 'pro-

2

gress', and such is still the magic of this prestige that Parisian novelties are liable to be more highly regarded than the products of serious talent which make their appearance in some other place. The double standard thus prevailing provides a yet further cause of critical confusion.

FORMERLY Paris set certain standards against which the attainments of other national schools might be measured. Since the beginning of the Second World War it has been the case only in a sharply diminishing degree; of recent years it has been true no longer. Where today British, Italian, American and other painters and sculptors working outside Paris are influenced by Paris, it is by the Paris of the masters, of the past, and little, if at all, by the Paris of today. There is for instance no painter at work in Paris today whose practice and ideas have so strong a hold upon the younger generation as those of the recently dead American, Jackson Pollock.

IN England the modern movement in art began in the least auspicious circumstances imaginable. So unfavourable, in fact, was the impression made upon Taine, a distinguished critic and an on the whole admiring visitor, by English painting at this time that he was driven to the conclusion that 'there is something wrong in the condition of the English retina'.[1] 'I do not believe,' he wrote in his *Notes sur l'Angleterre (1860–1870)*, 'that pictures so very disagreeable to look at have ever been painted.'[2]

The decades that followed the dissolution of the pre-raphaelite Brotherhood in the 'fifties were in fact the bleakest in the whole history of English art. Rossetti, Millais and Hunt survived, producing from time to time something to be valued, but their creative powers were in conspicuous decline. The great powers of Stevens were so misused as to bring him to a premature death with his greatest venture incomplete. Watts was a lofty yet self-contradictory figure, and Burne-Jones's gifts as a designer did not, except on rare occasions, redeem the languor and thinness of his imagination. The all but unchallenged power of the Royal Academy fostered almost exclusively the costume-piece and the anecdote. In an environment so pervaded by complacency and sentimentality, in which neither imagination nor the direct observation of nature nor interest in the problem of design or of the potentialities of paint played any part, where was a young painter of serious purpose to turn? The development of the art of painting during the nineteenth century, more especially during the latter half, was in the direction of the closest possible observation of life – the observation of it as an end in itself rather than as a means of nurturing some ulterior purpose. This was the direction in which the inner logic of painting was impelling it to evolve. There were two obvious sources from which a serious young painter growing up in the age of Alma-Tadema and Leighton might have gained some insight into the realistic impulse which was animating the great painting of his time. He might have looked at the masters of his own country, or he might have looked across the Channel. In 1860 Constable had been dead twenty-three years and Turner only nine. It is a strange fact that both these two masters of landscape, both long illustrious, should have had so negligible an influence upon the English school – a fact for which it is difficult to account. Both were admired abroad as well as at home; Constable, in particular, in France. They had, in fact, raised the reputation of English landscape painting to an eminence without precedent; foreign landscape painters, more especially those of the school of Barbizon, showed themselves in significant respects the followers in

---

1. *Taine's Notes on England.* Translated by Edward Hyams, (1957), p. 263.   2. Ibid. p. 263.

particular of 'the natural painter'. Yet what Englishmen followed in their footsteps? Certain writers have been inclined to exaggerate the influence of these two masters on their French successors, especially upon the impressionists. The aims of the two Englishmen were different from theirs. To represent, like the impressionists, 'a slice of life', more or less arbitrarily chosen, was no part of the programme of either. Constable tried to give a new naturalness by emphasis on 'light-dews-breezes-bloom-and-freshness' to a vision which had its basis in traditional canons of composition. Turner was a poet, but a poet whose creations had to carry conviction in an age of unprecedented scientific awareness. Both Constable and Turner could have yielded to a serious young painter ambitious to represent the life of his own time, in particular the landscape around him, a vast quantity of invaluable information.

If English painters were disinclined to study Constable and Turner they showed even more positive disinterest in the revolution in painting that was in progress in France. Because today Manet, the impressionists, Cézanne, Van Gogh, Gauguin and Seurat stand out (with Rodin) as the heroic figures of the second half of the century, it is easy to overestimate the positions (insignificant and peripheral) that most of them occupied during their lifetime. Among artists, however, news of major talents at work and especially of audacious innovation has a way of travelling fast, and English painters with minds attuned to the developments in France would have found means of learning about them. And it so happens that England was offered unique and continuous opportunities of understanding impressionism from early in the history of the movement. Far from availing itself of such opportunities, English critical opinion actually hardened against it: from an attitude more open-minded, even more sympathetic, than that often manifested in France, it became exclusive and hostile. This melancholy recession has been charted and documented in an illuminating essay by Mr. Douglas Cooper.[1]

In the first half of the nineteenth century contacts between French and English painters had been numerous and friendly. Lawrence was admired in France as he was throughout Europe; equally well known is the admiration of Delacroix for Constable and Bonington; Géricault brought his *Raft of the Medusa* to England, where it won a spectacular success, and where he painted his *Derby*. French progressive painters of a later generation accordingly looked to England in the confident expectation that their work would be understood – an expectation that persisted in the face of discouragement. A long succession of French painters came to England: Legros, who remained to become a British citizen, in 1863, Manet in 1868, and Fantin-Latour in the following year, while Monet, Sisley and Pissarro spent considerable periods here, where they painted many pictures of English subjects. Degas, Renoir, Toulouse-Lautrec, Gauguin, Van Gogh (before he began to paint) and Maximilien Luce were also visitors in England. Whistler, too, lived mostly in England after 1859. Through the initiative of the dealer Durand-Ruel, who opened a gallery at 168 New Bond Street between 1870 and 1875, London saw the first impressionist pictures to be exhibited outside France. During the early 'eighties Durand-Ruel renewed his attempt to interest British collectors in impressionism, and after an interval of more than twenty years he assembled, in 1905, a great collection at the Grafton Galleries, which included *Un bar aux Folies-Bergère* and *La Loge*.

The exhibition was the subject of controversy among artists and students and it was well attended, but the controversy quickly died away and a mere handful of the 315 pictures on view were sold: it made, in fact, a very slight impression. Several leading critics, among them Roger Fry, neglected

1. *The Courtauld Collection: A Catalogue and Introduction.* (1954).

4

even to comment on it. An attempt was made by Frank Rutter to acquire Monet's *Vétheuil: Sunshine and Snow* for the nation (which Durand-Ruel would have allowed him to buy for the sum he had collected, namely £160) but it was soon apparent that the impressionists were considered 'too advanced' and the project was abandoned. (The National Gallery not long before had declined the offer of a gift of a painting by Degas.)

After thirty-five years' exposure to impressionism – a mode of expression which owed something to England and which might have been expected to appeal to English taste – the English public dismissed it as an extremist craze.

THIS obstinate failure of comprehension had baleful consequences for the arts in Britain. A public which as late as 1905 had mistaken the great painting of the age for an ephemeral aberration – painting which had long been collected and honoured abroad, and long ceased to be thought of as revolutionary – was pitifully unprepared to understand the successive revolutionary movements which broke like waves upon the English shore. Barely five years after Durand-Ruel's impressionist exhibition there were shown two exhibitions consisting predominantly of pictures which were expressions of more recent and more radical tendencies: the first, held in Brighton in June 1910 and entitled 'Modern French Artists', consisted of 262 works by Cézanne, Matisse, Bonnard, Vuillard, Signac and others, the second in November the same year, entitled 'Manet and the Post-Impressionists', consisted of works that included 36 by Gauguin, 21 by Cézanne, and others by Van Gogh, Odilon Redon, Maurice Denis, Vlaminck, Rouault, Matisse and Picasso. This last was the celebrated exhibition assembled by Roger Fry at the Grafton Galleries.

The evolution of European painting after impressionism was a particularly complex process; the influences of Cézanne, of Gauguin, of Van Gogh, of Seurat, interacting the one upon the others, wove a pattern (affected by numerous other influences besides) sufficiently baffling even when all the evidence was accessible. But for the British public the evidence was fragmentary. Fry's exhibition inspired both exaltation and hatred; it opened many eyes; it seemed to open doors upon many possibilities; but the one thing it could not do was to clarify the inner logic of the development of European painting. The impact of this challenging but miscellaneous assemblage of pictures upon a public which only five years earlier had been unable to accept impressionism was deeply confusing. A symptom of the resulting confusion was the fury with which the exhibition was assailed. The view the exhibition fostered, that 'modern art' was perversely obscure and beyond comprehension, was one that long persisted and for some considerable time frustrated the growth of intelligent thought leading to reasoned convictions. Unlike the first, the Second Post-Impressionist Exhibition, also organized by Fry at the same gallery in October 1912, was an exhibition with a theme: Cézanne and his successors seen as exponents of a new classicism. The bewilderment of the public was further increased by this and by two other exhibitions: of 'Works by the Italian Futurist Painters' in March 1912 at the Sackville Gallery and a comprehensive collection of post-impressionist painting from Cézanne to young British contemporaries, brought together by Frank Rutter at the Doré Galleries in the autumn of 1913, in which an attempt was made to repair the relative ignorance of these painters, in particular, of the pointillists and intimists.

Within the space of three years the British public was made violently aware, and in a fortuitous and unhistorical manner, of European painting from Cézanne to the futurists. In the ensuing incomprehension Fry was the more readily able to impose upon a considerable and constantly growing section of the public his own evolving interpretation of modern art. Fry was an influential apostle of the concept of a reality beneath the evanescent appearance of things which it was the business of the artist to discover and express; not to 'seek to imitate form, but to create form; not to imitate life but to find an equivalent for life',[1] was how he once formulated, in an often repeated phrase, the central aim of the modern artist. A doctrinaire strain in his character impelled him at times to set values upon the work of artists who conformed to the ideas which he currently held that posterity appears unlikely to endorse, such for instance as Marchand, Lhôte and Friesz. This was conceded by his closest friends. 'I do think,' wrote Mr. Clive Bell in his affectionate yet candid study of Fry, 'he was inclined to give marks to pictures which, because they were right in intention, ought to have been right in achievement, and sometimes, I think, he was rather unwilling to recognise the patent but troublesome beauty of works that seemed to be sinning against the light.'[2] But it is not as a theorist that he made his most valuable contribution to the arts in England, for his ideas had mostly been anticipated by other writers, but as an inspired enthusiast for the visual arts endowed with a rare capacity for persuading others to share his enthusiasm. In this he was unapproached in his generation, unapproached indeed by anyone since Ruskin. In the last analysis it is by this power of evoking enthusiasm that the critic is to be valued. If Fry was inclined to over-rate minor artists because their practice seemed to confirm his ideas, so was Ruskin, and so was Baudelaire. It would not be difficult to call many of Fry's judgements in question, to show that his aesthetic was less original and less consistent than it seemed, to recall that his love of advanced art, even of the art of Cézanne himself, was of slow and hesitant growth. Not difficult, but neither would it be relevant to his greatest achievement: the principal part in the dispelling – in which George Moore, D. S. MacColl and others also played honourable parts – of the complacent disposition that had blinded the English public to the impressionists, in the incitement to a curiosity and a new delight in serious painting and sculpture. If to do these things is the end of criticism then surely Fry must be accounted a great critic. His immense authority was without recourse to any of the practices of the demagogue: he was not by nature eloquent, nor did he strive after eloquence; he made his impression by a persuasive combination of openness to or rather avidity for new illumination and of deep conviction.

BUT some four or five years before Fry established himself in England as the pre-eminent advocate of modern art, a modern movement in painting had begun to take shape. It is convenient to take 1905 – the year of Sickert's return from some five years' residence abroad, in Venice, Dieppe and elsewhere – as its point of departure. Back in London Sickert quickly became the leader of a group of younger painters, who foregathered in his studio at 19 Fitzroy Street. Writing in 1910 Sickert himself related how 'about six or seven years ago under the influence in France of Pissarro . . . aided in England by Lucien Pissarro and by Gore . . . I have tried to recast my painting entirely and to observe colour in the shadows.'[3] It is symptomatic of the strange indifference to impressionism that prevailed in England that one of the most enquiring and active minds among English painters, well acquainted with impressionism for many years, should have felt its full impact only when he was past forty years of age. Sickert was by disposition a crepuscular painter and very few of his luminist paintings rank, I think, with his finest. It may be that there was another, besides a temperamental, cause for his long retention of a low-toned palette. This was the influence of Whistler,

1. Preface to the French Section of the catalogue of the Second Post-Impressionist Exhibition.
2. *Old Friends: Personal Recollections*, (1956), p. 69.   3. *The New Age*, (26 May).

6

which may have delayed his adoption – as I fancy it delayed my father's – of an impressionist palette. However that may be, weary of his self-imposed exile, Sickert returned full of zest for the impressionists' enlargement of the possibilities of composition and full of zest, also, for London and for exerting his influence – he was an inveterate teacher – upon the gifted young men who were leaving the Slade School and – after a suitable period of probation – joining the New English Art Club, which had entered upon the last phase of the most influential period of its history.

The New English is intimately identified with a generation of painters whose reputations, with the exception of those of Sickert and, possibly, of Gwen John, are in the trough of the wave and at present accordingly excite little interest. In recent decades the character of the Club has not been easy to distinguish from those of several other exhibiting societies – a leading member not long ago was also concurrently a Royal Academician and President of the London Group. Members of the present generation find it difficult to appreciate what a predominant and for a while what a valuable contribution it made to painting in England.

It was founded in 1886 by English painters who had studied in Paris. (One of the names originally suggested for it was 'The Society of Anglo-French Painters'.) Whistler exhibited with the Club in 1888, and he served on the jury the following year. Works sent by distinguished foreigners – by Monet, for instance, in 1891 – were to be seen at the Club's exhibitions. The Club's original members were mostly practitioners of *plein air* painting according to Bastien-Lepage, but a more radical dissident group – to which control of the Club quickly passed – held in 1889 a separate exhibition under the name of 'London Impressionists'. In a militant introduction to the catalogue Sickert distinguished between the aims of the English impressionists and their French predecessors by disclaiming any wish 'to record anything merely because it exists', that is to say the more or less arbitrarily chosen 'slice of life'. On the contrary he clearly accepted 'beauty' as their aim, and he asserted that for painters the most fruitful course of study lay in a persistent effort to render 'the magic and the poetry which they see daily round them' (with especial emphasis, since they were mostly city-dwellers, on urban subjects). In an article written twenty-one years later he amplified his distinction between the original impressionists and their English followers. 'The pictures at the New English Art Club,' he wrote, 'are often described as impressionist. . . . This always surprises and amuses French visitors to England. A painter is guided and pushed by his surroundings very much as an actor is, and the atmosphere of English society acting on a gifted group of painters, who had learned what they knew either in Paris or from Paris, has provided a school with aims and qualities altogether different from those of the impressionists.'[1]

'The New English picture,' Sickert continued, 'has tended to be a composite product in which an educated colour vision has been applied to themes already long approved and accepted in this country.' Aware that the scale upon which the English group wished to work was larger than that which the pure luminism of the impressionists allowed, he was of the opinion that 'wherever we have been tempted to do impressionism on the scale of the exhibition picture, we have run considerable risk of being losers of the essence of what we had learnt from the French Impressionists'.[1] Influenced as they were by the impressionist palette, they evolved 'a method of painting with a clean and solid mosaic of thick paint in a light key'.[2] 'I doubt,' asserted Sickert, 'if any unprejudiced student of modern painting will deny that the New English Art Club at the present day sets the standard of painting in England. He may regret it or resent it, but he will hardly deny it.'[3]

1. "The New English and After". *The New Age*, (2 June, 1910).   2. op. cit.   3. op. cit.

For some twenty years the New English exercised a bracing influence upon English art: unlike the Royal Academy of those days, it welcomed and did not rebuff emerging talent. From about 1890 until about 1910 by far the greater number of serious painters were welcomed by the Club either as members or as exhibitors. The liberality of its outlook and the enthusiasm it generated drew to it generation after generation of the most talented of the younger painters. Whereas in earlier days pictures were apt to be judged by their subjects, the New English fostered a lively and intelligent interest in the art of painting itself. Gradually, however, the Club became vitiated by a spirit of complacency which in time hardened into intolerance. Because Sickert was a member, as well as their other mentor Lucien Pissarro (son of Camille), it was natural that the group which grew up round him after his return to London should have submitted their work to the New English in the expectation that it would be sympathetically received and that they themselves, like successive generations of their progressive predecessors, would sooner or later find places in its ranks. But Gore, elected in 1909, reluctantly became convinced that the Club had tacitly renounced its liberal and pioneering policy; Gilman's work and that of friends whom he admired was rejected. For a time, however, the Fitzroy Street group weighed the advantages and the possibilities of winning control of the Club, which still enjoyed great prestige with the public and among artists a unique measure of respect. Sickert advised that this was not possible; Gore and Gilman were of opinion that the Club had become, in fact although not in profession, an academic force and that its capture was accordingly not even to be desired. These discussions culminated, early in 1911, in the decision to form a new society, to be called the Camden Town Group, with Gore as President. The new society provided with a name and an organization the group of friends who during the past few years had formed the habit of meeting at the Fitzroy Street studio, and showed their pictures there to patrons – mostly of modest means – on festive Saturday afternoons. More significantly, it announced these friends' independence of the New English. Augustus John remained faithful to the Club, and Wyndham Lewis was shortly to inaugurate a movement of his own, based upon ideas sharply distinct from those evolved in Camden Town. Those who frequented 19 Fitzroy Street were drawn there as much by the exhilarating atmosphere of its gatherings, where new ideas about painting – almost all of them emanating from Paris – and their adaptation to their own purposes were discussed, as by anything in the way of an aesthetic held in common. There was, however, an inner circle united by something in the nature of a distinctive aesthetic, to which they gave the name of 'neo-realism'. This aesthetic was the result of assiduous experiment and constant discussion, and the general ideas upon which it was based were eventually formulated by Ginner.[1]

The 'neo-realists' of Camden Town conformed no more closely to any Continental form of post-impressionism than did the 'English impressionists' of the New English to impressionism.

They regarded themselves, first and foremost, as Realists, acknowledging impressionism as Realism's latest and most important manifestation. 'The impressionists, by their searching study of light,' wrote Ginner, 'purified the muddy palettes by exchanging colour values for tone values.'[2] Like the 'English impressionists' the 'neo-realists' rejected the impressionist concept of a picture as the representation of a chance glimpse of life begun and completed on the spot under the same effect of light. Their art, like that of the 'English impressionists', included comment upon and

1. Most comprehensively in an article entitled 'Neo-Realism', which first appeared in *The New Age*, and was reprinted as the foreword to the catalogue of an exhibition of paintings by Gilman and himself held at the Goupil Gallery from 18 April to 9 May, 1914.
2. 'Neo-Realism'.

interpretation of life. 'Each age has its landscape, its atmosphere, its cities, its people,' Ginner declared. 'Realism, loving Life, loving its Age, interprets its Epoch by extracting from it the very essence of all it contains of great or weak, of beautiful or of sordid, according to the individual temperament.'[1] Realism and luminism they shared with the impressionists, and with the post-impressionists – the great founder-generation of Van Gogh and Gauguin – they shared a more constructive, a less positively retinal, outlook on life. But it was a thoroughly traditional movement that was evolved by Gilman, Gore, Ginner, R. P. Bevan – who constituted this inner circle – for they not only disapproved of current developments in post-impressionism ('Voila l'ennemi . . . take away the rose pink and you find the Academic skeleton,'[2] warned Ginner) but also, for its scientific preoccupations, of neo-impressionism. When Sickert wrote of 'the carnival reputation' of Matisse, and of his drawing's 'exhibiting just the kind of school-facility that you do not find in good drawings or in great drawings',[3] he was expressing opinions from which most of his Camden Town friends would have been unlikely to dissent. In spite of certain principles held in common, the members of the group went their own ways as artists. Gore – whose gentle, serene nature and diplomatic talent held the Group together – was technically a highly traditional figure, who accepted, as Sickert observed, 'the instrument as he found it handed down to us by Monet and Pissarro', that is to say the impressionist instrument, which he first used working directly from nature. Under the influence of the post-impressionists, principally of Cézanne, he gradually aimed at a sharper, simpler definition of his planes. Although primarily a painter of landscape, urban and rural, and of the theatre, perhaps the finest of all his paintings, in both form and colour, is a portrait, *North London Girl*[4], of 1911. Gilman by contrast was a less complex but a more massive and deliberate figure: a painter who saw in terms of firm design, broad planes and colour of a splendid and forthright brilliance, in the service of deep emotion aroused by the spectacle of surrounding life: his lodgings, landscape, Mrs. Mounter, his charlady, whom he has made immortal, even his big, homely teapots. Of the Camden Town group of friends none so decisively rejected the sketchiness inherent in impressionist painting or was so determined to make his own the qualities of permanence and dignity. Even remoter from orthodox impressionism was Ginner: his paintings are devoid of atmosphere and as packed with detail at their thick pigment allows, and this often gives them an archaic look; yet few artists of his time have represented urban landscape with such intimate understanding. If his minute touch inclines to monotony, is there not compensation in what Sickert called his 'burning patience'? A lesser and until quite recently neglected painter belonging to the Group was Bevan, at his best as a painter of horses at horse sales and in cab-yards, a painter whose work has the same archaic look as Ginner's but who sometimes managed to express, through his gaunt forms and harsh simple colours, a moving compassion.

The Camden Town Group fostered a movement that was not revolutionary: impressionism was its point of departure and Cézanne, Gauguin and Van Gogh pointed the way ahead; it was a movement, rather, of logical evolution. Its conservatism must have been due in a large measure to the influence of Sickert. Critics have had occasion to notice inconsistencies in Sickert's opinions, but in one important respect these did not change. Again and again his writings and sayings testify to his conviction that painting was an integral process in which later painters extended, in various directions, the achievements of their predecessors; that the best painters of his own day were therefore

1. op. cit.   2. op. cit.   3. 'The Post-Impressionists'. *The Fortnightly Review*, (January 1911).
4. The Tate Gallery, London.

not superseding tradition but adding to it. 'We who know Poussin,' he wrote, 'can see how Degas follows on, normally, in most conservative order. We can see Pissarro evolve from Corot gradually.' Or again, 'I would invite the new French school . . . to consider for a moment that intellectual evolutions take more than one generation to deploy. One generation suspects a potentiality, the next hints at it. Tremulously the third stammers a few syllables, and so it goes on.' Or yet again, 'there can no more be a new art, a new painting, a new drawing than there can be a new arithmetic, a new dynamics or a new morality.' Gradually, however, the young painters' growth in the propitious atmosphere of Camden Town and the tensions set up by the increasing devotion of each of the members of the inner circle to a modern master – Gore to Cézanne, Gilman and Ginner to Van Gogh – led to a loosening of their ties with Sickert. For all his breadth of sympathy and his capriciousness Sickert was a man who was intimately identified with the well-established practices and ideas of his generation, and who moreover saw most naturally in low tones. His Camden Town friends, by many years his juniors, were, however circumspectly, moving away from the impressionism modified by English traditions which Sickert shared with Steer and Lucien Pissarro and most of their New English contemporaries, and were attempting to evolve styles of their own in the light of the teachings of their chosen mentors; and unlike Sickert they all saw most naturally in a high key. In the case of Gilman the steadily widening breach between Sickert and his Camden Town friends was somewhat exacerbated by a personal difference, but it was in essence the inevitable outgrowing of tutelage, and the tutelage of a man who differed from them temperamentally in an important respect. 'After his break of what was more or less discipleship with Walter Sickert and his plunge into the Signac palette and a brighter scheme of things,' Wyndham Lewis wrote of Gilman, but his words applied also to Gore and to Ginner, 'bitumen was anathema for him, and Sickert was bitumen. . . . He would look over in the direction of Sickert's studio, and a slight shudder would convulse him as he thought of the little brown worm of paint that was possibly, even at that moment, wriggling out on to the palette that held no golden chromes, emerald greens, vermilions, *only*, as it, of course, should do. Sickert's commerce with these condemned browns was as compromising as intercourse with a proscribed vagrant.'[1] Before they reached the fulness of their powers, however – but not before they had painted some of the finest pictures of their time in England – Gore and Gilman had died, the one in 1914 and the other five years later. Ginner lived on until 1952, developing little but rarely falling below the exacting standard that his 'burning patience' early prescribed.

In the history of art politics the year 1913 was crucial. The small groups of advanced painters that had grown up in the region around Tottenham Court Road during the preceding years were suddenly animated by a spirit of fusion. They were too small to be effective; their membership was largely identical and there was a consensus of opinion that it would be desirable to form a society which would enable progressive artists to face a hostile or at best an indifferent public with a measure of unity. The growing complacency of the New English, whose traditional enthusiasm for emerging talent had cooled, had become widely manifest, and the need for a new society to replace it was felt in many quarters. A meeting was held at 19 Fitzroy Street on 15 November with Sickert presiding at which it was resolved to found a new and comprehensive society, and to call it The London

---

1. *Harold Gilman, An Appreciation*, by Wyndham Lewis and Louis F. Fergusson (1919), p. 13.

Group. Gilman was elected President and he continued in office until his death. The London Group – its first exhibition was held in March 1914 – represented an amalgamation of the original Fitzroy Street circle, the largely identical Cumberland Market Group, and the vorticists led by Wyndham Lewis. The death of Gore, whose disinterested and benevolent nature, whose tact and charm, made for cohesion, released disintegrating tensions; the First World War brought further confusion, and the London Group came under the control of Fry and his friends; Bernard Adeney whom Rutter described as 'a blameless echoer in biscuit and pale-green tints of Cézanne's less successful nudes and landscapes',[1] succeeded Gilman as President.

In one respect the London Group did fulfil the aims of its founders: it became, and it still remains, the principal exhibiting society to which serious emerging talent turns with hope.

The predominant influence of Fry and his friends upon the London Group had one important and lasting effect upon the art world of London: it made a deep and permanent cleavage between those who were 'for' and those who were 'against' his Post-Impressionist exhibitions. When Fry was offered control of the Grafton Galleries he solicited the support of his friends among members of the New English – Steer, Tonks and my father among others – which they felt unable, mainly on personal grounds, to accord. When it became apparent that post-impressionism made so strong an appeal to the younger generation, by many of whom Fry was accepted as leader and prophet, it was only human that he should have borne it vividly in mind that he had given his old friends the opportunity of joining him and that, in his time of need, they had declined it. The effect of this situation was that these former friends were apt to be represented as reactionaries who had been shown the light and did not recognize it, and that, conversely, they themselves grew readier to scoff at flat-footed disciples of Cézanne and Matisse than to reassess their appreciation – respectful but not ardent – of Cézanne, for example, or to look at Matisse with wholly unprejudiced eyes. (I remember hearing in my father's house the kind of criticism of the impressionists – that their view of things in terms of colour rather than form involved the exclusion from their art of many of the qualities that characterized the art of the earlier masters – which was in harmony with the attitude of post-impressionists. The theories of Seurat attracted my father as little as those of Monet, yet in so far as it was the constant aim of his later life to combine structural design with brilliant colour he may properly be regarded as something of a post-impressionist himself.)

The breach which by the end of the First World War had come to divide the generation of Sickert and Steer and the generations who showed their work at the London Group was, I believe, deleterious in its effects. It made for the insulation of the older painters from the bracing climate of the 'twenties – less bracing, certainly, than that of the pre-war years, but quick with experiment and invention. It tended, moreover, to foster the notion among younger painters and the public that the art of their own time was without immediate antecedents – a notion that increased yet further the endemic confusion arising from the unchronological fashion in which the mainstream of modern art had become known in England.

THIS, then, in a telescoped and oversimplified form, is some account of the impact upon England of impressionism, of its obstinate rejection, of its eventual acceptance, in a radically modified form, by the generation of Sickert and Steer and their friends of the New English Art Club; of the gradual

1. *Art in my Time* (1933).

11

growth, after Sickert's return to London, of a movement among members of a younger generation which evolved, broadly speaking, from the 'English impressionism' of their seniors towards a conservative form of post-impressionism – intrinsically conservative, on account of its sobriety, however ardent the underlying emotion, and relatively traditional in comparison with what was afoot in Paris. While Gilman was painting his *Mrs. Mounters*, fauvism and the heroic phase of cubism had begun and ended. Value must not be equated with innovation, and in spite of the fact that their art was largely determined by their cautious assimilation of the teachings of post-impressionist masters several years in their graves, the best of the paintings of Gilman and Gore are contributions to European as well as to British art.

Not long before the First World War, however, a far more revolutionary movement, vorticism, erupted in England. Vorticism was primarily the consequence of the provocation offered to a readily provoked painter – shortly to become a critic of literature and the visual arts, philosopher and novelist besides – Wyndham Lewis, by a series of spectacular incursions by the *Duce* of futurism, Marinetti. The original Futurist Manifesto had been published in *Le Figaro* of 20 February, 1909, exalting machines, speed, youth and war, 'the only health-giver of the world'. In the course of the campaign which it announced Marinetti lectured in London in March and April of 1910 at the Lyceum Club. The futurists' international exhibition arrived from Paris and was shown at the Sackville Gallery in March 1912, and in the same month Marinetti lectured at the Bechstein Hall. His campaign in London was renewed in November 1913 when he lectured at Hulme's 'Poets' Club' and in April and May 1914 at the Doré Gallery, and on 7 June, with Nevinson, he published in *The Observer* a pronouncement entitled 'Vital English Art', which became known as the English Futurist Manifesto. Lewis was at once attracted and repelled by the futurists. 'We applaud', he wrote, their 'vivacity and high spirits', but 'the effervescent Action-man of the futurist imagination would never', he maintained, 'be a first-rate artist . . . there is no reason why an artist should not be active *as an artist:* every reason, rather, why he should. Our point', he concluded, 'is this: the artist *cannot* have to the full the excellent and efficient qualities we admire in men of action, unless he eschews action and sticks hard to thought.'[1] In spite of his conviction that the artist should be the man of action only in his art Lewis saw the possibilities of the futurists' militant technique. This, accordingly, he adopted. The second Futurist Manifesto, of April 1909, had called for the conversion of salons into fields of battle; he assembled 'a determined band of miscellaneous anti-futurists' to barrack Marinetti. 'Mr. Epstein was there; Gaudier Brzeska, T. E. Hulme, Edward Wadsworth', he wrote. 'After a hearty meal we shuffled bellicosely round to the Doré Gallery . . . Marinetti . . . put down a tremendous barrage in French as we entered. Gaudier went into action at once. He was very good at the *parlez-vous*, in fact he was a Frenchman. . . . The Italian intruder was worsted.'[2]

From July until December 1913 Lewis had been working at Fry's Omega Workshops. This organization, and the militant methods and manifestos of the futurists, must have impressed him with the desirability of agencies for the propagation of his ideas and the advertisement of his activities. In the spring of the following year he founded, with Miss Kate Lechmere, the Rebel Art Centre at 38 Great Ormond Street and in June appeared the first of the two numbers of what Pound, in a letter to Lewis, called 'the great MAGENTA cover'd opusculus', *Blast*.

At the Rebel Art Centre it was intended that classes, lectures and exhibitions should be held.

---

1. *Wyndham Lewis the Artist* (1939), pp. 144, 145.   2. *Blasting and Bombardiering*, by Wyndham Lewis (1937), pp. 36, 37.

Associated with it were, among others, Etchells, Gaudier-Brzeska, Wadsworth, Epstein, Nevinson, Bomberg, Hulme and Pound. It cannot be said of this project, as it can of so many others, that it was extinguished by the First World War. It came to an end after an existence of barely four months, because it was unable to withstand the stresses imposed upon it by the possessiveness with which Lewis regarded it, and by his consequent suspicion of the intentions of his associates. Its activities were effectively publicized, but it disappointed the hopes of its friends. Marinetti and Ford Madox Hueffer (afterwards Ford) gave lectures there, and only two persons sought to enroll as students: a man who aspired to improve the design of gas-brackets and a lady pornographer.

Although it survived only two numbers – No. 1 was published on 20 June 1914, and No. 2, War Number, in July the following year – *Blast* was a more spectacular undertaking. This big 12″ by 9½″ periodical, announcing the Great English Vortex, was a largely iconoclastic manifesto. Its most novel feature was a series of editorial 'blasts' and 'blesses'.

Only nine years had passed since impressionism was dismissed with contempt and less than four since post-impressionism provoked an uncomprehending uproar. Known only to a numerically insignificant section of the public, the most advanced painting in England was being carried on by little groups of painters chiefly round about Tottenham Court Road. A number of Victorian popular-academic painters were alive, some of them esteemed and active still: Marcus Stone had seven years to live, B. W. Leader nine, Luke Fildes thirteen and Frank Dicksee one year more. In spite of the substantial achievements of the New English impressionists – now half-forgotten, of the Camden Town and associated groups, of Fry's exhibitions at the Grafton Galleries, English art was still largely smothered in Victorian complacency and sentiment. One of the aims of *Blast* was to blast it away. 'We do not want the GLOOMY VICTORIAN CIRCUS in Piccadilly Circus,' it declared editorially. Its bellicose satire was directed also to less obvious ends: to the exaltation, first and foremost, of a classical – in a particular sense which Lewis elaborated and clarified in successive publications – and a militantly masculine view of art, which involved an indictment of futurism for its hysteria and its adolescent machine-worship. It is hardly possible to estimate the effects of *Blast*, for the sound of this robust explosion of irony and affirmation was lost in the continuous rumble that was soon heard all day from across the Channel. *Blast*, nevertheless, marked the end of an epoch. It marked the sudden end of English provincialism where the visual arts were concerned. Those who had contributed most to the enlightenment of English public opinion from Whistler to Fry had done little more than add to its understanding of the greatest modern school of painting, the French. They were bringers of good news, preachers of a gospel. There was news and a gospel of which England stood urgently in need; and to bring the one and to preach the other was the most valuable task they could perform. But by 1914 their efforts had borne fruit: there had come into being a small section of public opinion which had assimilated what they taught. *Blast* did not – except incidentally – expound: it criticized. It did not tell its readers in adulatory terms what the futurists and the cubists were about; it told them where they were wrong. There had always existed, of course, a lunatic fringe ready with blind abuse of anything 'French', but there had never been, unless I am greatly mistaken, such searching and such aggressive criticism from an English pen of contemporary art movements abroad. The criticism of cubism remains valid to this day; futurism offered an easier target.

Reference to the aesthetic of *Blast* involves an obligation to mention the debt of Lewis to the young philosopher T. E. Hulme. Hulme was an apostle of classicism in the special sense in which Lewis also understood the term: against the naturalistic 'vital' art produced by the romanticism of the modern world he set up the classical ideal of the archaic Greeks, the Egyptians, Indians and Byzantines, 'where everything tends to be angular, where curves tend to be hard and geometrical, where the presentation of the human body, for example, is often non-vital, and distorted to fit into stiff lines and cubical shapes of various kinds'.[1] It is difficult to assess precisely the intellectual relationship between Hulme and Lewis, but we know that it was shortly after the ideas propounded by Hulme began to make themselves felt in London that Lewis's own drawing assumed a geometrical non-vital character, and much in his writings suggests a heavy debt to Hulme. Others, besides Lewis, were affected by Hulme, among them Epstein, whose bronze *The Rock Drill*,[2] of 1913, may well owe something to his ideas, so completely does it fulfil them.

In the visual arts, then, the nine years or so before the First World War were years of exceptional activity. Earlier generations of New English painters had thrown out a resounding challenge to the shabby smugness, the portentousness so oddly combined with triviality, that characterized the Royal Academy and the whole official attitude towards the arts; they had reminded the public that painting was a serious calling; their juniors in Camden Town, within a narrower circle, had made a like demonstration: and the arts had pursued their course to an accompaniment of mounting excitement, and by the eve of the War it would seem that more people felt more passionately about the arts in England than they had since the days of Ruskin. There was a plethora of talent coming forward. The arts were less isolated from one another than for many years. London had had opportunities of seeing the most advanced painting and sculpture – Kandinsky in 1909 and 1910, and Brancusi in 1913 – at the Allied Artists, which held a series of immense exhibitions at the Albert Hall and had been brought into being by Rutter in 1908 in imitation of the Paris *Indépendants*. Suddenly there was a public to whom the arts mattered: there were fights between futurists and anti-futurists; fantastic intellectual night-clubs sprung up. The best-known of these, The Cave of the Golden Calf which belonged to Madam Strindberg (the third wife of the dramatist August Strindberg), had walls 'relevantly frescoed', according to Sir Osbert Sitwell,[3] by Lewis, and the columns supporting the ceiling were by Epstein; vorticist dances were danced, and vorticist evenings held, at one of which, it was announced, 'the Manifesto of Rebel Art will be read to the sound of carefully chosen trumpets'.[4] London was not to be compared for creativity with Paris, where during the early years of the century a new and revolutionary art was being shaped by a crowd of men of dazzling and various gifts. But London was provincial no longer; here too gifts abounded, and as in Paris there prevailed widespread confidence that momentous events were taking place, and that events more momentous still were impending. 'A ferment such as I have never since felt in this country', wrote Sir Osbert Sitwell, 'prevailed in the world of art.'[5] Then came the First World War, dispersing the men working to such purpose and extinguishing their hopes.

The war had one consequence for British artists to mitigate despondency at the interruption of their profession and to incite some of them to memorable activity. This was the policy adopted first by the British and later by the Canadian Government whereby artists were sent to work as artists in the

1. *Speculations, Essays on Humanism and The Philosophy of Art*, by T. E. Hulme, edited by Herbert Read, 1936, p. 82.
2. The Tate Gallery, London.   3. *Great Morning* (1948), p. 208.   4. Violet Hunt, *I Have This to Say* (1926), p. 214.
5. *Great Morning*, p. 235.

various theatres of war. The original intention was no doubt that they should be employed to stimulate patriotic sentiment by glorifying the fighting services and to make records that would complement the writings of historians. But whatever the intention behind it, the policy was interpreted with enlightenment and courage – an enlightenment and courage surprising in view of the melancholy character that for the past century had marked most officially commissioned art. The privilege of working at one of the various 'fronts' was not confined to the illustrious or the respectable; a number of young painters, unknown to the general public, were also appointed as official artists. Not only was the selection of artists good; so was the liberty with which they were permitted to interpret their assignments. To send out artists, free to represent what they saw in accordance with their own sensations and convictions, to send men to places where killing and destruction were being organized, and this on a scale without precedent in the whole blood-letting history of mankind, was a magnificent enterprise. It was an enterprise justified by bringing into being a unique picture of war. The iconography of war is probably almost as old as war itself, but the artists who have represented it have been in the main concerned to represent it in conformity with the wishes of their patrons, or as patriots and propagandists and moralists, or as the makers of factual records. There have been exceptions, and splendid exceptions. Goya's *Disasters of War* – to recall the most famous – were uncommissioned expressions of an artist's horror at the shame of war; so too were Callot's more conventional *Miseries*. The fact that Goya was a greater artist than any of those who depicted the First World War does not detract from the uniqueness of their description of it. A considerable number of men of widely differing outlook were given unusual facilities for observation and left free to interpret what they saw in accordance with the dictates of their individual natures. They produced at once the most comprehensive and the most searching description of war that had ever been set down on canvas and paper, touching every aspect of it except, perhaps, the spectacularly heroic. They owed, of course, much to their subjects, most of all to the Western Front, the vast stretch of scarred, burnt, poisoned, nightmare battleground and graveyard far more terrible than any imagined Armageddon. Many of them responded with startling ardour to the challenge of their subjects, some showed depths of emotion and technical resources of which they themselves had previously been unaware, and which, with the return of peace, they discovered that they possessed no longer. To others their experience brought sudden maturity. Paul Nash, for instance, a young watercolourist of somewhat pre-raphaelite tendency, with a predilection for decorous park-like landscape, created image after image of great originality and power, and Nevinson, the single English representative of futurism, was briefly possessed as never before or afterwards of an imaginative fury. The best works of the War Artists are apt to be lost to view among the vast and miscellaneous accumulations of the remotely situated Imperial War Museum in Lambeth; were this not so, they would be recognized as meriting a place among the best British art of the half-century.

THE remarkable fact about the success of the War Artists' mission is that it was won in opposition to the general trend of painting. There are not many generalizations about modern painting which are of wide application, but it would be true to say that the most continuously potent factor in its evolution has been – and remains – a progressive recoil from anything approaching representation of the world of appearance; a progressive rejection of normal vision. There has been a corrosion of confidence in the visible world and in the validity of our perceptions of it. The necessity for the clearly recognizable representation of life involved in the War Artists' mission called, therefore, for a temporary reversal of this potent trend. Much of the finest war art, however, was the work of artists who were susceptible to the magnetism of the abstract. In the case of the most uncompromisingly abstract English artist, however, Wyndham Lewis, the effect of the war was to provoke a lasting recoil towards a style which would allow him to represent subjects of wider human concern. 'The geometrics which interested me so exclusively before,' he wrote, 'I now felt were bleak and empty. *They wanted filling.*'[1] The effects of Lewis's experience as a War Artist were exceptional: the contact with surrounding life, fostered by intelligent official patronage, did not – except while the war was being fought – reverse the trend away from naturalistic representation and during the succeeding decade the corrosion of confidence in the visible world was more than ever conspicuous.

IN a study of an individual artist a writer is able, at propitious moments, to approach and to illuminate the centre of his creative activity, but in a study of a period it is otherwise. A period – even the most conformist period – is a stretch of time during which many different kinds of artists are active, many movements are ebbing and flowing and clashing one with another. A period – at all events before the great figures have decisively emerged – is a vast flux. General histories of contemporary art are too often written in a manner which suggests that the persons treated of played their parts as though on a stage. The artists singled out in the present anthology were not always the most widely admired artists of their time, and I am well aware that they may not be those destined to find most favour with posterity.

The two decades which separate the two World Wars are a particularly intractable period. Almost all the important figures of the first half of the century were active, and there was an energetic and complex interaction of movements which derived an initial vigour from the exhilaration that followed the making of peace. It seems to me that the division of painters into categories that would do least violence to the facts would be to place in the first those who were mostly connected, either as members or exhibitors, with the New English Art Club; in the second those who shared to a greater or lesser degree the critical doctrines advocated by Fry; and in the third those who belonged mostly to a still younger generation and who reacted against the aesthetic purism taught by Fry in favour of values other than plastic.

OF the first the most illustrious member was Steer, a painter with a rare understanding of the potentialities of oil paint and of watercolour, a massive figure, conservative in the most honourable sense, who, although wholly dedicated to his vocation, was excluded from a place with the masters only by a besetting spiritual and intellectual supineness, but whose early figure subjects – a few of the finest of which could hang without dishonour beside the finest works of the impressionists – the epic landscapes of his early middle years and a single portrait proclaim him to be one of the considerable painters of the century. Well below him in the esteem of his contemporaries but far above in that of the present generation was Sickert, his complement. One of the most intellectually gifted artists of his age, capricious, curious, witty, he was able to compensate with his intelligence and application for his lesser natural aptitude for the handling of paint in a long series of pictures which successfully challenge comparison with those of the more magisterial Steer. Other members of the group were Ethel Walker, who attempted, often with success, the difficult undertaking of fulfilling the claim of Camille Pissarro that impressionism was a way of seeing compatible with the free play of the imagina-

1. *Rude Assignment, a narrative of my career up-to-date*, by Wyndham Lewis (1950), p. 129.

16

tion; Pryde, a creator of fantastic ruins, and his brother-in-law William Nicholson, that rare pheno-menon in the modern world, a little classical master, who is apt to be underrated by a generation which prefers the heroic failure to the completely achieved but minor success. (Neither Pryde nor Nicholson was a member of the New English, but they may be considered alongside its members according to the very rough classification used here.) Another was Rothenstein, who early in the century sacrificed the felicities of style which had brought him early success and attempted with the whole force of his ardent yet austere nature to come to closer and closer grips with the world of appearance. Another, Augustus John, already acclaimed as one of the great draughtsmen of the age, was an uneven painter but in his best work displays an energy and an audacity and a zest for life that makes the work of other men look supine and cautious beside it. 'Nature is for him like a tremend-ous carnival,' wrote Wyndham Lewis in a review of an exhibition of paintings made by John in the West Indies before the Second World War, 'in the midst of which he finds himself. But there is nothing of the spectator about Mr. John. He is very much a part of the saturnalia. And it is only because he enjoys it so tremendously that he is moved to report upon it.' The quotation gives an indication of the artist's attitude towards his subject. Gwen John was in almost every respect her brother's opposite: he is a dazzling improviser; she was methodical. He is exuberant; she was concentrated, subdued, sad. Celebrity came to him during his student days at the Slade; she was known only to a few friends and her work did not arouse sufficient interest during her lifetime to inspire a single article. Yet today her painting begins to be spoken of with greater admiration than her brother's, for its simplicity, its breath slowly attained without loss of its rare intensity. Gwen John exhibited occasionally at the New English, but she was never a member of it, or of any other organization – except the Catholic Church. Other leading figures within what I have termed the New English group were Lucien Pissarro, a painter who carried on, without genius but with reticence and seriousness of purpose, the tradition of his great impressionist father; McEvoy, a portrait painter able to make portraits of women that have a poetry and distinction very rarely to be found in portraits of the fashionable; Tonks, a painter of rectitude and charm, and Orpen, an artist of extraordinary natural endowments – some experienced judges rated his student drawings more highly than John's, and some of his early paintings seemed to announce a new master – whom, however, spiritual aridity and the want of a lucid and enquiring intellect, capable of the 'funda-mental brain work' which Rossetti postulated as necessary for the artist, prevented from giving more than fragmentary expression to his vivid and personal sense of life. A member of the same generation, but an isolated figure, an Irishman, who did not attain his full powers until late in life, was J. B. Yeats, who created with enormous audacity and zest a nostalgic dreamlike picture of Irish life and legend.

Most of these painters lived on until the 'thirties, 'forties and 'fifties (one of them is indeed active still), and several of them made some of their best pictures late in their lives. As individual painters they retained – with the exception of the almost unknown Gwen John – the high repute they had won early in their lives; but although interest in their art ebbed and flowed, it mostly ebbed. They continued to inspire respect, though less lively emotion, as new painters, new movements and com-binations, became successfully the focus of excitement.

THE influence of Fry, especially over the young, established by the two post-impressionist ex-hibitions but arrested temporarily by the war, re-asserted itself strongly during the early years of peace. He was able to exert a wide measure of control over the London Group, and over the critical sections of *The Nation* and its successor *The New Statesman and Nation*. Both his own writings and those of his entertaining and militant disciple, Mr. Clive Bell, in these journals – to which they were both frequent contributors – and elsewhere were read with merited attention. The critical ideas of Fry underwent continuous development in harmony with his own susceptibility to the experimental, in harmony, too, with ideas which he imbibed in or from Paris. The core of his aesthetic, however, remained constant.

'The one constant and unchanging emotion before works of art,' he wrote, 'had to do always with the contemplation of form and this was more significant spiritually than any of the emotions that had to do with life.' The ideal of which he was so deeply convinced and of which he was so persuasive a champion was the ideal of an exclusive and all-sufficing beauty inherent in form, colour, rhythm and texture. Any significance beyond these that a work of art might happen to possess was for Fry irrelevant to its significance as a work of art, even perhaps undesirable as a distraction from the contemplation of its essence.[1] Today when successive generations have been guided by very different ideals and when there may be seen in the theories of Fry some confusion of means with ends, it is well to bear in mind that the insistence upon the syntax and grammar, upon the indispensable constituents of painting, may well have been for many painters salutary in its effects. The influence of Fry was for a time so preponderant, and he was so successful in focusing the reverence of several generations of young English painters somewhat exclusively upon Cézanne, that Cézanne's establishment as their 'tribal deity' has come to be so completely accepted as one of the inevitable facts of history as to preclude almost everyone from ever envisaging the possibility that history might have taken a different course. A rare exception is Mr. Robin Ironside, who has deplored the fact that Fry's 'rousing analyses . . . should have directed attention upon the patient manipulation of volumes that was a feature of Cézanne's method rather than upon the rich, repining vision of a primitive elysium that flowed from Gauguin's very essence', and that 'the way was thus paved for the emulation of the art of Matisse, Derain, Vlaminck – rather than that of Chagall, Rouault or Chirico to which the native temper might have been more easily attuned'.[2]

If the effect of this preponderant authority upon some painters resulted in a fruitful concentration on, so to say, the language of painting, it led other painters out of their way. A notable example was Gertler. Under the influence of Fry's predilections in post-impressionism his work gained in solidity and concentration in design, but it lost the precisely focused intensity, the glowing actuality that distinguished his very early works inspired by the life of the Whitechapel ghetto. The two painters whose work Fry found most sympathetic were Duncan Grant and Vanessa Bell. All three were united in close friendship, and she was married to Mr. Clive Bell. The precise degree to which Grant was affected by Fry's aesthetic purism and by the outlook of the circle of highly intellectual friends whose views on aesthetics were predominantly formed by Fry is difficult to determine, but Fry himself had the discernment to see and the candour to admit that the aesthetic in which he so passionately believed might inhibit the living British painter whom he admired the most.

'It was perhaps inevitable,' he wrote, 'that, coming at a time when the movement of creative artists was in favour of insisting almost exclusively upon the formal elements in design, he should have tended to suppress his natural inclination to fantastic and poetic invention.'[3] It is sufficient to my

1. The most succinct statement of Fry's views is to be found in his essay 'Retrospect' (1920) in *Vision & Design*.
2. *Painting Since 1939* (1948), p. 12.   3. *Duncan Grant* (Hogarth Press), 1923, p. viii.

present purpose merely to indicate that although Grant's intellectual predilections made him intermittently responsive to the aesthetic doctrines of his friends his most personal gifts were not only for the poetic invention noted by Fry but for the representation of the real world, in particular of the richness of colour and the weight and texture of things. Vanessa Bell was the possessor of a like gift, which manifests itself more robustly but on a smaller scale and with simpler themes.

For many young painters the influence of Fry was liberating: it gave them confidence to disregard much in the art of their time that was as inferior as it was highly esteemed; it brought near to them the exhilarating events and personalities of the Paris art world; but upon mature painters his influence was apt to be effective in inverse ratio to the stature of the painter concerned. Grant, as has already been noted, his intimacy with the critic notwithstanding, was to some degree resistant to his teaching; about those (and they were many) who harkened uncritically to the beguiling voice and gave themselves over to the creation of an art of exclusively plastic values – which was not in practice readily distinguishable from the manufacture of Cézannes or Matisses – the less said the better.

English mistrust of dogma, English interest in the ebb and flow of surrounding life, opposed the widespread adoption of the aesthetic purism preached by Fry, which was in any case more talked of than practised, and which proved more effective as an incitement to artists and critics to examine their ideas than as an authoritative guide to practice.

THERE flourished, as was therefore to be expected, painters who owed much to Parisian example and ideas, but in whose art the subject played a larger part than purists could approve. Among these the first was Matthew Smith, whose contacts with France were not second-hand but direct: he went to Brittany in 1908; in 1910 moved on to Paris where he worked briefly at the short-lived school which Matisse ran, and during the next twenty-nine years he continued to live largely in France. The originally somewhat hesitant temperament of Smith received its impetus and authority from Matisse and his fellow fauves. His early work – such, for instance, as his two *Fitzroy Street* nudes, of 1916 – appeared to be the expression of an intellectual, a constructive, a sometimes melancholic and essentially a draughtsman's vision; but between 1922 and 1926 he evolved a vision – and a method appropriate to its expression – of a quite contrary kind, a glowing vision in which passion and intuition play the dominant parts and in which the operations of the intellect count for little, the vision of an impassioned painter and an indifferent draughtsman. The paintings of Smith, entirely devoid of literary overtones though they are, are not simply exercises in what used to be called 'significant form', or even significant colour: they may rather be regarded as reckless, rhetorical hymns of praise to the warmth and opulence of the real world. In a long series of landscapes, still-lifes and nudes Smith has shown himself the most authoritative and personal English exponent of fauvism, but without the note of stridency, of hysteria even, of the most characteristic productions of this school and of the northern expressionism with which it had close affinities and connections. The fauvism of Smith is an opulent fauvism nourished and mellowed under a southern sun.

Also in debt to the School of Paris yet with affinities with the third group presently to be discussed are others for whom the exclusive aesthetic of Fry was restrictive, namely Wyndham Lewis, William Roberts and Paul Nash, all of whom began to make reputations shortly before the First World War, which they consolidated in the course of it and during the years that followed the peace. The distinction between them and those who accepted Fry's aesthetic was that their pictures were primarily images rather than exercises in plastic values.

Lewis began as an abstract draughtsman of the most uncompromising kind – so uncompromising that he sharply criticized the cubists, especially Picasso, for founding 'their invention upon the posed model, or the posed Nature-Morte, using their models almost to the same extent as the impressionists', and thus for avoiding invention.[1] During the First World War Lewis repudiated this uncompromising attitude. Had it not been for the War, this repudiation would have been delayed, but 'War', he wrote, 'and especially those miles of hideous desert known as "the Line" in Flanders and France, presented me with a subject-matter so consonant with the austerity of that "abstract" vision I had developed, that it was an easy transition.'[2] Another cause for this repudiation is to be found in the humanistic interest generated in the writing of his first novel, *Tarr*. Roberts was likewise preoccupied with the creation of his sardonically humorous pictures, close-knit and lucid, of cockney life. Paul Nash was always preoccupied with imagery, with which at certain times he may be said to have been obsessed. This is not to suggest that all three artists were not also fully alive to plastic values. Roberts and Nash would no doubt have subscribed to the opinion expressed by Lewis: 'I can never feel any respect,' he wrote, 'for a picture that cannot be reduced, at will, to a fine formal abstraction.'[3] Nash shared, then, with Lewis, the conviction that a picture should be primarily an image rather than a formal construction, but their imagery was of a contrary character. That of Nash was subjective; he took a delight in irrational fantasy which could verge occasionally on whimsy. His was not a mind from which imagery flowed naturally, but it was a mind deeply devoted to and deeply versed in the imaginative tradition: he accordingly developed his intense receptivity and systematically exposed himself to poetry, prose and the visual arts in their most imaginative aspect, in particular those that were most evocative of the earth's oldest memories.

For the decade, or thereabouts, following the end of the First World War, there were many painters, including a number of the most gifted, who rejected, explicitly or tacitly, the purist contention that the absolute beauty inherent in plastic values is somehow diminished or compromised unless the artist cultivates it to the exclusion of all other beauties. A painter whose work was an unconscious challenge to this purism was Stanley Spencer. One or two of his earliest paintings, most noticeably his *Apple Gatherers*,[4] of 1912, reveal a yielding to post-impressionism. But the yielding was only momentary. No considerable English painter active during the half century under review has been so negligibly affected by the School of Paris as Spencer; none indeed has occupied so isolated a position. He owes something to Masaccio and to Fra Angelico, and a little more to a master of the Northern tradition to which he himself belongs, the elder Brueghel, but his work may be vainly scanned for any but insignificant traces of contemporary influence. For Spencer a picture is an image to which all those elements which for Fry were the ends of painting are merely means. The imagery which has most powerfully obsessed him has been religious, but particularly before the Second World War it has also been intermittently sexual. There is another obsession which plays a part in his vision not less important: his native village of Cookham. He has painted other places and painted them with imaginative insight – most notably Macedonia in his Burghclere *Resurrection* – but Cookham is one of the springs, perhaps even the mainspring, of his art; cut off from its influence, though it might have flourished for a year or two, it would eventually have withered. It may be a parochial judgement, but it seems to me that as a religious painter Rouault alone among his contemporaries shows

1. *Blast II.*   2. *Rude Assignment*, p. 128.   3. *Blasting and Bombardiering*, p. 129.   4. The Tate Gallery, London.

a comparable power of compelling the beholder to accept his images as valid images, the events he depicts as events which in truth took place. Critically, however, the honours – in spite of the achievements of Lewis, Nash or Spencer – rested mostly with the purists, who were favoured by the *zeitgeist* subtly and lucidly interpreted by Fry, and on a more popular level by the lively and combative Mr. Bell, who pointed, assiduously by way of confirmation of their theories, to the honourable figure of Grant as well as the illustrious master of Aix.

The kind of painting in fact fostered by the teachings of Fry – classic examples of which were to be seen year by year at the exhibitions of the London Group – had in practice for its subjects the traditional subjects of European realistic painting, that is to say, landscape, interior, still-life and portrait. It differed from painting of the more conservative kind in that plastic features such as recession and projection, the interplay of planes, the functional as distinct from the ornamental use of colour, were given an insistent and often an awkwardly self-conscious emphasis. Clearly implicit, however, in the conception of an all-sufficing beauty residing in plastic values alone was the justification for an art from which recognizable subjects would be excluded. In art, as in other spheres of creative action, that which serves no purpose withers and is eventually discarded. Fry did not advocate the exclusion of the traditional repertory of subjects from the work of art, but he did teach that in so far as subject was not simply a pretext for the creation of significant form and colour it was irrelevant, and in so far as it claimed any degree of attention on its own account it was intrusive. It was clearly in accord with the doctrine of plastic self-sufficiency that the subject, which lingered on precarious sufferance, without any positive part to play and indeed a possible source of infection, would have to go. And go it did from the work of an ever growing number of painters and sculptors. Abstract painting had made its appearance on the Continent of Europe with Kandinsky around 1910 and in England some three years later with Wyndham Lewis, whose *Planners* must have been among the first drawings from which subject was entirely eliminated. As has already been noted, this initial abstract movement in England had petered out, repudiated by its principal exponent and advocate, and when abstraction revived in the early 'thirties and on an altogether more substantial scale it was from Continental precursors that it derived its inspiration. The teachings of Fry had nevertheless – however unwittingly – prepared the way for the acceptance of the far more radical ideas and practice of Kandinsky and Mondriaan.

FAITH in the value of imagery, impaired by the sterilized ideal of self-sufficient, plastic beauty, was reasserted in the later 'twenties and the 'thirties in an extreme and often irresponsible form by surrealism, whose exponents attempted to exploit the imagery of the unconscious mind, in particular the possibilities of free association first employed for clinical purposes by Freud. It was this preoccupation which gave rise in their art to one of its most conspicuous features, namely the juxtaposition of incongruous images. The claims made by the surrealists for their finds in the mysterious depths of the unconscious, impossible as they were to verify, and the ridiculous fashion in which the affairs of 'official' surrealism were conducted alike alienated serious minds. 'I believe the moment is at hand,' wrote Dali in 1930, this spectacular movement's most spectacular exponent, 'when by a paranoiac and active advance of the mind, it will be possible (simultaneously with automatism and other passive states) to systematize confusion and thus to help discredit completely the world of reality.' Neither such a programme as this nor the painting of the man to whom it might be said, as Victor Hugo wrote to Baudelaire, 'You create a new shudder', could be expected to find wide acceptance in sober England, but the surrealists' reassertion, with such lucidity and vigour, of the primacy of the image did find an answering echo. It accordingly offered a challenge to what Dali called, in 1935, 'this model debility called abstract art'.

Abstract artists show a solidarity and a capacity for organization which is in the sharpest contrast to the proscriptions and grotesqueries of the surrealists and the overriding individualism of painters in general, so that their influence is greater than either their number, the impressiveness of their total achievement compared with that of their figurative contemporaries, or the vulnerability of their aesthetic would lead one to suppose. These advantages were demonstrated by the vicissitudes of the Seven and Five Group. This society was formed in 1919 and it had as its initial inspiration a conscious recoil from the aesthetic purism of Fry and a conscious sense of the importance of imagery. Among early members were Ben Nicholson, Evie Hone, Christopher Wood, Winifred Nicholson, David Jones, Frances Hodgkins, Henry Moore, John Piper and Edward Bawden. In the 'thirties owing, it would appear, to the energy and influence of Ben Nicholson – who early in the decade had turned towards abstraction and was to become the movement's most consistent and accomplished English exponent – the Society changed direction. Frances Hodgkins resigned, apparently on a disagreement with the new policy of favouring abstract art, and since 1935 or 1936 the Society has been defunct, though never formally disbanded.

By this time there were symptoms of the emergence of a new generation of painters and draughtsmen convinced of the importance of subject, as well as of a new generation who willingly accepted the restrictive limitations of abstract painting. To the one belonged Christopher Wood, a painter both lyrical and sinister and a born colourist, who was helped and encouraged by Picasso, but who died young, David Jones, Ivon Hitchens, Edward Burra, William Coldstream, Victor Pasmore, Ceri Richards, and Graham Sutherland; to the other Ben Nicholson, Barbara Hepworth and, briefly, John Piper. But for the second time during the period summarily sketched here developments full of promise were frustrated or diverted by war.

In certain respects the impact of the Second World War upon the arts resembled that of the First. Once again official patronage of a courageous and discriminating kind brought into being a many-faceted record of the several fields of action and – not less impressive – the fields of civilian action behind and beneath; it offered artists the opportunity of serving as artists in the capacity that made the best use of their talents. And once again it was not on the whole the realists who raised the most impressive memorials to the great armed clashes, to the vast dislocation of society and of individual lives; it was rather those who had on the whole been disposed to neglect the ebb and flow of life in favour of the cultivation of the imaginative vision or else of formal aesthetic values.

The Second War affected the course of painting even less than the First. It was barely four years before the First began that Great Britain had felt the full impact of the revolutionary movements in progress abroad, and even then the impression they made had been confused. The younger artists had mostly not taken a definite stand, and so it came about that their art was more susceptible of change than would have been likely later in their lives. The First War transformed Wyndham Lewis from an abstract artist into one preoccupied with his subjects; Nevinson from a high-spirited experimenter in progressive adventures into – temporarily – a painter *engagé*, and likewise Paul Nash, previously a gently poetic exponent of the English water-colour tradition brought somewhat up to date by a cautious infusion of the contemporary spirit. Who would have expected any of these to have made the terrifying chaos of the Western Front into great art? Certainly not the authorities, perceptive though they were, for none of the three was in the first instance selected as a war artist and all had their first sight of the war as soldiers on active service. But in the Second War (and with the experience gained in the First to be drawn upon) the response of artists to their subject was rather less unpredictable. By 1939 the revolution in art was established: artists mostly knew where they stood in relation to it, and surprises were accordingly fewer.

The Second War did, however, hasten a change, perceptible just before its outbreak, in the work of the most considerable artist to emerge since the First, Henry Moore. As a sculptor and draughtsman he had from his earliest days been passionately preoccupied by form and space, and this preoccupation and his ardent admiration for early sculpture of many kinds, its bold simplifications, its primitive simplicity and power, fostered in him a concern with formal values which appeared at times to be exclusive. But he has always been conscious of the force of other motives. 'Abstract qualities of design,' he wrote, 'are essential to the value of a work, but to me of equal importance is the psychological, the human element.'[1] Early in the war, 'quite against what I expected,' he confessed, 'I found myself strangely excited by the bombed buildings, but still more by the unbelievable scenes and life of the underground shelters.' On his return home from his subterranean visits he drew them from memory. 'I somehow felt drawn to it all. Here,' he wrote, 'was something I couldn't help doing.' The effect of the scenes of the shelter world brought his humanism to a new and grander consciousness. For the expression of humanistic values the European tradition provides the most appropriate language, and its appropriateness for the expression of the emotions stirred in him by the shelter world became suddenly apparent to him. 'It was not until the Blitz in London,' he said to a friend, 'that I began to realize how deep-rooted the Italian influence had been . . . the Mediterranean tradition came once more to the surface.' Masaccio's frescoes in the Carmine, ever one of the prime sources of his inspiration, had suddenly an enhanced relevance. 'There was no discarding,' he added, 'of those other interests in archaic art . . . but rather a clearer tension between this approach and the humanistic emphasis.'[2] The fact that humanism played so impressive a part in the work of the foremost artist of his generation gave imagery an enhanced importance in the eyes of his younger contemporaries. In the shelter drawings, of which he made about a hundred, and in the two sketchbooks in which he noted down his original impressions, Moore created a memorable world peopled by figures at once monumental and ghostly, encompassed by vast shadowy spaces, all brought to a vibrant life by the depths and brilliances of his colour.

THE greatest change in the art world of Great Britain brought about by the war affected not, in the first instance, the producer but the consumer. As has already been noted, the British public had not been precisely unfriendly to the visual arts – it had attended the major exhibitions in considerable numbers – but it had been lethargic, and more interested, on the whole, in the old than the new, towards which an attitude of suspicion, if not hostility, lingered until the first year or so of the war. Then the public seemed to be quite suddenly transformed. The change was as pervasive as it was mysterious. Could it have been that the people who knew that they stood, for the time, alone between the nazi nightmare and everything that the world held precious had experienced a curiosity about some of the good things that belonged to the kind of civilization they were fighting for? Or

1. 'Henry Moore, Sculpture and Drawings', 1949, p. xxxix.   2. These four quotations are taken from Henry Moore, an interview with James Johnson Sweeney. Partisan Review (March–April 1947).

could it have been that the fact that each night might have been their last caused many to reflect that it would be sad to die without having read Shakespeare, listened to Beethoven, seen a Rembrandt? Or was it that shortage or deprivation of amenities which had formerly been readily available made people value the arts more highly? Whatever the cause, the results were manifest everywhere, whether in an increased demand for the cheap editions of the classical authors, an increased desire to listen to the classical composers and to see fine painting and, in particular, new painting. A single example will suffice to illustrate the change as it affected my own corner of the world. By 1942 the Tate Gallery had been made unfit for exhibition purposes by damage from bombs, and the authorities of the National Gallery had placed a group of their own rooms at our disposal. A friend asked me what we proposed to show there. I explained that the Tate's collection had continued to be built up, and that in particular a considerable number of works by younger British painters, unrepresented in the Tate before the war, had been added to it, and that it was proposed to show these new acquisitions. 'At a time like this,' he said, 'who'll come to look at them except a few lonely intellectuals?' Such crowds came to see these pictures, which before the war would have been dismissed as 'highbrow', that we had to ask for police to help to marshall them.

This expansion of public interest in the visual arts – which has since been maintained and even quickened – has diminished the sense, which often depressed the spirits and impaired the initiative of immediately preceding generations of artists, of spending their lives in the making of things unwanted and of little concern except to a few like-minded friends. The public at large now interests itself in painting and sculpture to a degree unequalled during the century, and although taxation has thinned the ranks of the great collectors – who in general show little interest in the art of their contemporaries – a large number of smaller and in the main discriminating collectors has appeared, and public authorities have shown themselves prompter than ever before to recognize what they believe to be emerging talent. As a consequence of these developments many talents have been welcomed and fostered which in rougher times would have withered; indeed the artistic life of Britain since the war has been impressively vigorous and varied.

It is impossible within the limits of this Introduction to treat except in the most general terms even of the leading figures among the crowd of painters of originality and talent who are active today, of whom some appeared before the war and others are of more recent growth. The simplest and least misleading procedure would be to classify them according to their relation to the 'normal vision' upon which the oldest and most consistent of living European traditions, namely realism, is based. This classification would distinguish three groups: those who gladly accept the validity of 'normal vision'; those who accept the world of appearances as the exclusive subject of their art but reserve, or rather insist upon, the right to alter it, even to transform it, in the interest of the visionary eye or of aesthetic preference, and lastly those who reject it in favour of the appeal of an exclusive and all-sufficing plastic beauty. There has been continuous interaction between members of these groups; there have been desertions, recruitments, conversions; yet each group is animated by an elaborately evolved and tenaciously held idea. In their essence these underlying ideas remain distinct: they might be personified respectively by, for example, Coldstream, Bacon and Ben Nicholson.

By the end of the war nearly all the realists, most of them associated with the New English Art Club, who had already reached maturity by the beginning of the period sketched in these pages, had died: Gwen John in 1939, Steer and Sickert in 1942, Rothenstein in 1945; but Nicholson lived until

1949, Ethel Walker until 1951, while Augustus John is happily active still. By an odd coincidence with the exception of Ginner, who lived until 1952, their successors, Gilman, Gore, Bevan and the romantic water-colour painter J. D. Innes, predeceased them, as the post-impressionists, Van Gogh and Gauguin, predeceased the impressionists. Several younger realists, mostly the friends and students of their New English or Camden Town predecessors, were fruitfully active, Allan Gwynne-Jones, Edward le Bas, W. G. Gillies and Ruskin Spear notable among them.

But today realists face a peculiar difficulty: that the public, or at least large and influential sections of it, is reluctant to interest itself in life represented according to normal vision. Whether it approves of it or not, the public has been deeply affected by the intense and often violent vision of those who have looked at life in a highly idiosyncratic way; and it is not easy to persuade a public familiar with Van Gogh, Munch, Seurat, Rouault, Braque, or Picasso, to look with the same interest at Courbet and Manet (even if it rates them more highly than their successors), and *a fortiori* at the realists of our own time. This is true not only of that part of the public disposed to welcome what is new; it is true even of the lunatic fringe which makes occasional disturbances at avant-garde exhibitions and writes letters to the newspapers pleading for 'sane art' and 'sincere work'. Those members of it who visit art galleries are more often to be discovered in the modern rooms in hysterics in front of Picasso and his contemporaries than in the quiet enjoyment of the beauties of those earlier realists in whose names they protest against the art of the present. The reluctance of the champions of tradition to take opportunities of enjoying the painting for which they proclaim their love has been strikingly apparent, for example, from their almost ostentatious absence from exhibitions of a traditional character held at the Tate; from the Exhibition, for instance, of Sir Henry Tate's Foundation Gift, in 1947, or from the Pre-Raphaelite Centenary Exhibition, in 1948, or from the G. F. Watts Exhibition, in 1955. There is indeed much to be urged in criticism of the art of the present, but it is an art in its finest manifestations marked by so much originality and so much energy as to make it a magnet which draws its detractors with scarcely less power than its admirers.

Today even realists, therefore, are often impelled to be realists with a difference; to rethink their aesthetic in relation to abstraction, for example, or to the proper function of photography or to the social functions of art. There have been of recent years two attempts to bring into being realistic movements adapted to today's conditions. The first, which took shape just before the war, was made by Victor Pasmore, William Coldstream, Graham Bell and Lawrence Gowing – a group which became known as the Euston Road School (after the small school they briefly conducted in that street). It involved the recognition that a great tradition had lately flourished and for no compelling reason been abandoned, and an attempt to build something new upon the basis which the impressionists and Sickert had bequeathed. The attempt was shortlived – it culminated in an exhibition at Oxford in 1941 – but the best painting the School produced was marked by high purpose and distinction; Pasmore's paintings of the Chiswick reach of the Thames on which he lived announced him as a reincarnation of Whistler, adding to that master's diaphanous dreamlike vision of London's river a fuller range of colour and a capriciousness of accent entirely personal to himself. The revived realism of the time produced nothing finer, either in England or anywhere else, to my thinking, than the best of Pasmore's landscapes, *The Wave*,[1] of 1939–44, for example, or *The Quiet River*,[2] of 1943–44, *Chiswick Reach*,[3] of 1943, *Winter Morning*,[4] and *The Gardens of Hammersmith*,[5] of 1944.

1. Coll. Sir Kenneth Clark, K.C.B.   2. Coll. Lady Herbert.   3. The National Gallery of Canada, Ottawa.
4. Coll. Sir Kenneth Clark, K.C.B.   5. Coll. Mr. Hugo Pitman.

Scarcely less beautiful are his figure paintings made during the same years, the *Nude*,[1] of 1941, or *Girl with a Curtain*,[2] of 1943.

No single event so well illustrates the precarious hold of realism over the minds of serious painters today than Pasmore's enthusiastic abandonment of it in the late 'forties. No work of Pasmore's in whatever convention is without signs of the rare gifts of its maker, but his abandonment of the world of normal vision has involved the sacrifice of powers of lyrical observation unique among his contemporaries. A few years earlier Pasmore had been preceded into abstraction by another realist, Rodrigo Moynihan, a painter whose unusual powers of construction are manifest in his large and ambitious *Staff of The Royal College of Art*,[3] of 1951, but who subsequently returned to Abstraction.

The second attempt to adapt realism to the special conditions prevailing today is so recent that it is difficult to assess. The roughness of the liberties its exponents take with nature, their disregard, for instance, of the laws of perspective, the arbitrariness of their colour, made me hesitate to call them realists and consider whether their place is not, after all, with the brilliant but amorphous group to which I shall presently refer, who take the actual world as the basis of their art yet insist upon the right to distort it, in one interest or another, to any extent. Jack Smith, Edward Middleditch, Derrick Greaves and John Bratby are realists in the sense that their distortions seem to be made neither in imaginative nor aesthetic interests, but in the interest of enhanced actuality. They are 'realists with a difference', realists more akin to Van Gogh than to Courbet, but it is perhaps only by such toughness that realism can reassert itself, can regain its hold upon the public interest. But it is by no means certain that the movement will continue: the strange robustness – a robustness which seems almost to verge upon the epileptic – of Bratby still seems realistic in intention, but Smith is already susceptible to the magnetism of the abstract.

The vision which takes its subjects from the visible world, not as they are but as they are transformable by imagination, has a far stronger hold, especially in England, than traditional realism. Indeed it is the way of seeing of most serious British painters at the present time.

THIS way of seeing – which was, of course, the way of seeing of earlier painters, Lewis, Nash and many others – assumed a new authority in the later 'thirties and during and after the war in the figure drawings of Moore, especially the shelter drawings, the fallen trees and rock landscapes of Graham Sutherland and the architectural landscapes of John Piper. For a brief time these three artists were thought of as leaders of a neo-romantic School, and their work was exhibited together. Before long it was realized that three unusually gifted contemporaries happened to be at work, and that no new school was in process of formation. Indeed the differences between them were soon observed to be so radical that their names ceased to be linked. Moore has continued to develop the humanism first perceptible in the late 'thirties and magnificently proclaimed in the shelter drawings. Sutherland, who had begun as a disciple of the Palmer of the visionary Shoreham years, has been increasingly affected by the School of Paris and he delights in rocks, thorns and other of the harsher features of nature as a kind of symbolism expressive of a pessimistic view of life not untouched by cruelty. He has also painted a small number of highly dramatized portraits. The reception accorded to these portraits aptly illustrates the preference of the public – even of the more conservative part of it – for the modern idiom, involving radical distortion in response to the dictates of the artist's inner or outer eye. Sutherland is the first British painter to apply with full force the contemporary idiom –

1. The Tate Gallery, London.   2. Coll. Mr. J. Wyllie.   3. The Tate Gallery, London.

which he himself has applied with conspicuous success to landscape – to the human face, above all to the illustrious human face. The public of today looks at 'straight' portraiture with indifference – even a portrait by Augustus John, whom Sutherland's most fervent admirers would probably concede to be a finer portrait painter than he, arouses respect rather than enthusiasm – yet the exhibition of each successive portrait by Sutherland is almost a national event.

A less massive figure than Moore, a less vehement and energetic than Sutherland, Piper has many virtues diffused among a range of activities unique among his English contemporaries: he is not only a painter and draughtsman who has practised both abstraction and romantic topography and innumerable variants between these extremes, but he is a designer of stained glass, and for the theatre, and a writer on many topics. Some day a retrospective exhibition will enable us to see this protean and delightful personality in the round. Obviously personalities as strong as these three affected their contemporaries, in particular their younger contemporaries – John Minton and John Craxton, for instance, were for a time in debt to Sutherland – but the most important way in which they influenced the art of their time was by the force of their imaginative interpretation of the real world. Influence, however, was not exerted in one direction only: Francis Bacon, a painter of great imaginative power, who focuses his attention upon subjects and themes from which normal men prefer to avert their eyes, has long been admired by Sutherland with manifest consequences for his own work. Bacon showed little natural aptitude for painting and never received formal instruction, but with the audacious cultivation of his sinister imaginative gifts has little by little come the ability to use paint to such purpose that it is even on occasion a delight in itself. Other imaginative painters who owe more to Continental surrealism than to the example of their British contemporaries are Edward Burra, a satirical portrayer of low-life and of the macabre, Tristram Hillier and John Armstrong. Roy de Maistre has applied a rigorous cubist discipline to the interpretation of contemporary and religious subjects. Other notable original interpreters of life – simply to name painters whom I myself particularly admire – are David Jones, Ivon Hitchens, Cecil Collins, L. S. Lowry, Edward Bawden, Joseph Herman, Ceri Richards, William Scott, Lucian Freud, Alan Reynolds, Albert Houthuesen, Alan Davie and Peter Lanyon, and the Scottish painter John Maxwell, whose work the English public has too few opportunities of enjoying.

These, then, are the chief among the large and extremely varied group of painters who subscribe neither to realism nor to abstraction, and who maintain the right to alter normal appearance to any extent this side of intelligibility in order to emphasize the communication it is their purpose to make. There is hardly need to comment on how very different these painters are from one another: nothing could be more different from the painter of Salford, L. S. Lowry, England's only true provincial master, than the painter of Camelot, David Jones, a portrayer of legend and myth of the rarest poetic gifts; or from the sombre, robust scenes of miners' and peasants' lives of Josef Herman than the tense, unquiet stillness of Lucian Freud; or from the discreetly and elegantly stylized landscape of Edward Bawden than the ardent fluidity of Ceri Richards' imagination – an imagination nourished both by surrealism and abstraction. So various are these painters that to classify them as a single group is, of course, to minimize the radical differences between them, but they hold, in fact, this one aim in common: they are all of them concerned to make communications – some of them explicit statements, other vague allusions – about the nature of life. In their aim of specific communication they differ from realists, who represent what they see in the faith that they may reveal something of the very essence of life which appearance expresses or conceals, and from abstractionists, whose purpose it is neither to 'imitate' nor to communicate but to create plastic values without reference to the world of appearances, which shall be valid in their own right.

So compelling and so pervasive is the influence of abstraction that many besides abstract artists are affected by it, but there flourishes in Great Britain today a distinguished group of pure abstract painters; compared with the two categories already outlined it is not large, but although the general public remains indifferent it grows both in numbers and in prestige. Its foremost exponents are Ben Nicholson, Victor Pasmore, S. W. Hayter and Rodrigo Moynihan. Nicholson is one of those temperaments, comparatively rare, which, though far from insensitive to the beauties of the visible world, is moved by an innate tendency towards abstraction in its purest form. He expresses himself with a perfect naturalness in a language which others have to cultivate. There are abstract painters militantly active today who, we may reasonably assume, had they been active instead between, say, 1880 and 1910, would have been engaged in the attempt at the photographic representation of silver birches or of heather. It is his natural command of abstraction, and his taste and his clarity of view, which distinguishes Nicholson from those who are abstract painters merely because fashion has made them so. Pasmore, having repudiated the realistic vision which his gifts of eye and hand enabled him to realize with such rare authority, has shown, in the practice of the cold and restrictive art of his adoption, all the fervour of the convert. He first became an abstract painter; then, abandoning the medium he was born to use, he has of recent years preferred to work in plastic. Nothing he makes is without distinction, but it is difficult for a lover of painting not to regret his conversion. The subtle and agitated abstract vision of Hayter finds even more eloquent expression in engraving, of which he is the foremost teacher in Europe, than it does in painting. Moynihan's history as an abstract painter falls into two apparently disconnected phases. He was a member of a group consisting of the gifted but regrettably short-lived Geoffrey Tibble, its most active spirit, Edgar Herbert and Graham Bell, who developed between 1933 and 1937 an abstract style characterized by broad, loosely painted brush-strokes. They contributed to an exhibition of 'Objective Abstractions' at the Zwemmer Gallery in the Spring of 1934. This movement seems to have had little or no direct influence upon the abstract impressionism practised today. Yet how strikingly it anticipated one of the later movement's principal characteristics! Moynihan himself, in the catalogue of the Zwemmer exhibition, claimed that his paintings 'have more in common with the impressionist technique whereby painting identifies itself with, and derives from, its means, than with a system in which the artist imposes on his canvas a preconceived idea'. After an interval of more than twenty years as a realist – and a traditional realist at that – Moynihan has subsequently resumed his practice of an abstraction of a not dissimilar kind.

The work of art from which any reference to the world of appearance was strictly excluded and which appealed only to the aesthetic sense was widely regarded until a few years ago as the ultimate expression of the recoil from realism. By some indeed it was even regarded as the ultimate expression – the highest achievement or the *reductio ad absurdum* – of the revolutionary urge that has animated modern art. More recent developments have shown those who held this opinion to have been mistaken. The revolutionary impulse has not slackened, and during the past decade a mode of painting has been developed in comparison with which the painting of, say, Ben Nicholson appears replete with bourgeois virtues – with traditional attributes, that is to say, that members of the younger generation have discarded. The elaborate composition that distinguished the best of the following of Mondriaan, for instance, is the most conspicuous absentee. Pierre Soulages, one of the leaders of this newest movement, has disclaimed all precise intention, and has stated that he is 'guided by . . . a longing for certain forms, colours, materials, and it is not until they are on the canvas that they tell me what I want. It is what I do that teaches me what I am seeking.' Intention has likewise been disclaimed by Sam Francis, another eminent exponent. 'I believe that the value of an action (painting) lies in the realm of the unintentional.' The emphasis in this emerging art – variously manifest in action painting, abstract impressionism, other art and *tachisme* – is rather, as the first of these terms suggests, upon the painter's impact upon his canvas, upon the actual pressure of brush, palette knife or hand, and the quality of the paint itself, than upon the final result distinct from these, or more precisely upon the artist's gestures and his materials envisaged *as* the result, upon the most intimate identification of means with ends. There is little of the earlier pedantic exclusion of imagery – Dubuffet, a pioneer, and Appel, a prominent member, of the movement make use of it – only a general sense of its irrelevance. Of the currently existing movement's pioneers, none, I think, is British, yet it has found here numerous converts, some of them gifted and sustained by a sense of liberation from all exterior disciplines, even from the architecture which marked earlier non-figurative works.

There is one respect in which *tachisme* is not revolutionary painting, but rather the most extreme manifestation of a movement with a longish history. One of the most persistent impulses behind modern art is the determination that the material used shall be seen for what it is and enjoyed for what it is, and not be forced or beguiled into looking like something else, into being a means of deception. 'Truth to material' was the expression often used to describe this conception. The painting of Ingres, for example, is manifestly in conflict with it, for the imagery of this painter could be realized almost as well in enamel or watercolour. The painting of Van Gogh, on the contrary, is in strict conformity with it: his imagery is conceived in paint, and his thick, furrowed pigment never loses its nature. But with Van Gogh the medium, however aggressively undisguised its nature, is strictly subordinate to the painter's imagery. With the *tachiste*, I take it, the medium together with the natural handwriting of the painter takes control, and by their joint effect deeper forces are considered to be brought into play, and the picture, as a physical object, is not to be strictly distinguished from the acts by which it is made.

I have made particular mention of this very recent movement, at the time of writing scarcely ten years old, because it seems to point the direction which experimental painters are taking, but I make no claim to have brought it into focus, or to be able to distinguish with any degree of clarity men and women of original feelings and ideas from their plausible followers, and I have accordingly selected few examples of it for inclusion among the illustrations.

*　　*　　*

After the Renaissance sculpture fell for some centuries into a decline which even the occasional appearance of sculptors of genius, such as Bernini or Houdon or Alfred Stevens, was unable to arrest. By the nineteenth century in England understanding of sculpture had dwindled so far that the difference between Stevens and the common run of official sculptors was only tardily perceived. Only a few years after Stevens, a sculptor of a genius so commanding that his contemporaries, however reluctantly, were compelled to accord him recognition made his appearance on the other side of the

Channel. It is no denigration of the great masters of his generation, the impressionists, to recall that, revolutionaries though they were, they were also the heirs to a tradition which was as continuous as it was splendid. Rodin had no such tradition to shape or to nourish his art: he had to look back as far as Donatello, Michelangelo, and beyond them to the sculptors of the Middle Ages and to the Greeks. The man who looks to remote sources for inspiration is exposed to dangers, of which antiquarianism is perhaps the most insidious, from which the heir to a continuous tradition is relatively immune. In spite, however, of his isolation and the incomprehension he had to meet, and all the hostility and neglect that incomprehension breeds, Rodin not only fulfilled, in the course of a long and unremittingly industrious life, his own vast potentialities, but in so doing he woke sculpture from its long dogmatic sleep transformed. History may well recognize Rodin as the greatest master of his age; it will assuredly recognize him as its most potent and pervasive influence – an influence which may be seen by its effects upon men whose temperaments and gifts are in such sharp contrast to his own as, for example, Picasso and Matisse. Even more important for the well-being of sculpture than the specific teachings of Rodin was the atmosphere of confidence and audacity which he imparted. It is hardly possible to measure with any degree of precision the extent of his pervasive influence, but it is surely not by accident that Rodin was immediately followed by a whole succession of sculptors of unusual powers: Maillol, Despiau, Epstein, Lehmbruck, Brancusi, Moore and Giacometti, to name at random a few of the most notable, to say nothing of the great painter-sculptors, Renoir, Matisse, Modigliani, Picasso. (About the sculpture of Degas little is yet certainly known, but he presumably began to model in the middle 'sixties independently of Rodin.)

In no country had sculpture become more debased than it was in England at the beginning of Victoria's reign. Stevens appeared, but his countrymen proved unworthy of him, and he was harried to death with his finest achievement, *The Wellington Monument* in St. Paul's Cathedral, incomplete. At the turn of the present century the best that England could show were the dignified and scholarly but languid and meagre bronzes of Havard Thomas. The energizing effects of Rodin's achievement were not felt in England until Epstein, who settled here in 1905 and began a few years later the long series of busts that proclaimed him the foremost portrait sculptor of our time. No other portrait sculptor can compare with him either in dramatic interpretation of character or in mastery of form. In spite of the virulent opposition provoked by his work until quite recent years he completed more public commissions than any other independent British sculptor of the present century. In his earlier years in England Epstein – although the greater part of his work is within the tradition established by Rodin – was much affected by sculpture produced most notably in reaction against it, that of Brancusi, as well as by such related ideas as, for instance, those of the anti-romantic philosopher T. E. Hulme. Primitive sculpture played a significant part in his formation, as it did in that of many of his contemporaries. *The Tomb of Oscar Wilde*,[1] of 1912, and *The Rock Drill*,[2] of 1913, both illustrate Epstein's susceptibility to such influences, and how well they could serve his purpose. As he grew older he became less susceptible to influences such as these, although sufficient traces remained to mark him as a man belonging to a later generation than his master. Considering Epstein's outstanding powers, his influence upon his British contemporaries has been surprisingly slight. Several possible explanations come to mind, but the most likely is that Epstein's contemporaries had already learnt directly from Rodin – long greatly admired in England – what

1. In the Cemetery of Père Lachaise, Paris.   2. The Tate Gallery, London.

they wished to learn of what they could learn, and that the rising generation looked for guidance, especially after the two Post-Impressionist Exhibitions, not to the impressionist generation to which Rodin belonged but to the post-impressionists, who were mostly in reaction – however respectful – against what he stood for. Had Epstein continued in the line of *The Rock Drill* he would probably have become the leader of a British School of post-impressionist sculptors, but remaining mostly within the Rodin tradition, he became, although a potent, a somewhat isolated figure. Epstein's emergence was followed by that of three younger sculptors of note, two of them English, Eric Gill and Frank Dobson, and one, Gaudier-Brzeska, born in France, who spent his brief but incredibly productive working years in England.

Gill was an impassioned and accomplished craftsman, an ardent though not uncritical convert to Catholicism, and a man of wide range but exact ideas. One important, indeed essential, qualification of a sculptor in the round was lacking in Gill, namely a sense of solid form, and this explains his preference for carving in relief. *The Stations of the Cross* in Westminster Cathedral, carved during the First World War, and the slightly later series in St. Cuthbert's, Bradford, show with what dignity, fervour and precision he could express himself in the flat, almost heraldic style that he evolved early in his life as a sculptor. That he was on occasion able to master the complexities of carving in the round is evident from *Mankind*,[1] of 1937–1938, and a handful of other examples. Graham Greene has observed that 'a new repository art grew up under his influence', but his influence was not, fortunately, limited to such a melancholy end. Gill was a man of a radical and logical cast of mind, ever concerned with first principles, and when these seemed to require it ever ready to make new beginnings. Fanatical dislike of the superfluous embellishment of nineteenth-century sculpture and of the remoteness of the sculptor himself from the act of making sculpture, which was either cast from moulds or carved from models by studio assistants or commercial firms, provoked Gill to evolve a style so simple as to be almost primitive, and to carve the stone with his own hand. 'Stone carving is *conceiving* things in stone,' he said, 'and conceiving them as made by *carving*.' His example and his blunt and lucid advocacy gave immense impetus to the practice of sculptors' carving their own sculpture. Dobson was a slightly younger contemporary, who began as a talented but somewhat conformist post-impressionist – his brass head of *Osbert Sitwell*[2] is an admirable example of his early work – but who has of late years lost something of his energy and his impulse to enlarge or to deepen his experience. Because his work appeared at one time to justify certain fashionable post-impressionist presuppositions, this excellent sculptor was treated as though he were a great master – in a monograph on his work a distinguished critic called him 'one of the three most interesting sculptors in the world since the middle ages' – but his reputation will no doubt recover from the overpraise which is reputation's most dangerous ordeal. (If only ambitious artists who solicit or even eagerly suffer the too fervent advocacy of influential critics would remember the risk they are courting of sorrow in their old age and disappointment for their heirs!) Two other sculptors of note, younger members of the post-impressionist generation, were Leon Underwood and John Skeaping, both notable in particular for their intelligent assimilation of the pervasive influence of negro sculpture, which was based not so much upon imitation as upon insight into the sources of the awe-inspiring vitality of primitive artists.

But of all the post-impressionist sculptors at work in England Gaudier-Brzeska, who packed a lifetime's work into some three or four years of inspired and ceaseless industry, was the most

1. The Tate Gallery, London.   2. The Tate Gallery, London.

31

phenomenal. He was born at St. Jean de Braye, Loiret, the son of a woodcarver whose ancestors are said to have carved some of the figures on Chartres Cathedral, and he first came to England to study business at Bristol University; at the age of twenty he settled in London, where he mostly lived until he returned to France to be killed in the First World War. His talent matured almost as soon as it showed itself, and although his poverty-harassed life was erratic his ideas were rounded and balanced. He succeeded in relating his preoccupation with form ('I shall derive my emotions solely from the arrangements of surfaces, the planes and lines by which they are defined,' he wrote) with his conviction that nature formed the basis of art, that the artist should not, as he put it, 'invent things instead of translating them'. It is difficult to place the art of Gaudier-Brzeska in relation to the other sculptors of his time, for his talents were so extraordinary and the time afforded for their widely varied exercise so brief; had he lived and continued as he began he would have become a master.

THERE emerged in the early 'twenties a sculptor who was within a few years to transform the climate in which British sculptors work and to give a lustre to British sculpture which it had not enjoyed since the Middle Ages. This was Henry Moore, who, although only eight years younger than Under-wood and actually Skeaping's senior by three years, ushered in a new epoch. He began as a by no means non-conformist figure, in the sense that he rejected outright the academic conception of sculpture and based his own art upon archaic models, studied mostly at the British Museum. In describing him as a conformist figure I intend, of course, to convey that the object of his conformity was the system of ideas – by the 'twenties widely accepted by many serious artists – evolved by the post-impressionists, which for a sculptor meant the rejection of a large part of the system of ideas for which Rodin had stood – a rejection, of course, not inconsistent with the fullest recognition of the greatness of Rodin's own work and of his successors' indebtedness to his example – the rejection more especially of Rodin's impressionism, his emphasis on the dramatic and, on the technical side, of his practice of employing workmen to do his carving instead of carving himself, and of attempting to coerce stone into resembling substances wholly unlike itself, most often flesh, and thereby – it was contended – violating its natural properties. Before long, however, Moore began to emerge as a sculptor of great and ever-growing authority. His debts to his masters: the ancient Mexicans and Egyptians, the Negroes, Giotto, Masaccio and Picasso, he has never sought to disguise or even to minimize; he has on the contrary proclaimed his gratitude. Moore can afford this magnanimous but by no means invariably followed course, for year by year the originality of his art has become more manifest.

The decisive revolutionary movements in modern art owe far more to painters than to sculptors; sculptors have in general been content to accept – with whatever power and originality – ideas which have originated with painters. Like the other sculptors of his time Moore has looked attentively at contemporary painters, in particular at Picasso, but he has evolved sculpture that is more independent of contemporary painting than that of any British sculptor and more original.

Some of Moore's sculptures have the appearance of abstraction, but the intention behind even the most abstract of these has not been to create a form valid in itself and without reference to nature but to penetrate to an inner reality, to provide, perhaps, analogies for certain principles of structure, growth, erosion and rhythm. The greater part, however, testifies frankly to his interest in life and most of all to his interest in his fellow human beings. For all his rejection of the classical, he is in one

32

sense at least conspicuously classical himself, in his indifference to the individual and in his concern with such general conceptions as the Family, Mother and Child, Warrior, even generic Man. There is nothing intimate about the art of Moore, not even in the relations between his mothers and their children. His figures, like all his forms, are massive and hieratic; they do not suffer the frets and stresses of common life, rather do they just serenely exist in their remoteness. Inert and massive though they are, Moore's figures possess a latent, primeval power, as rare in modern sculpture as it is common in that of primitive people. Unlike Picasso or Klee, Moore is a man of a few simple slowly but logically evolving ideas, chiefly concerning certain fundamental aspects of man and nature, which he has expressed with a simplicity that is the result of complexities not avoided but resolved, and with a memorable strangeness.

Moore's illustriousness – no other English artist since Sir Thomas Lawrence has enjoyed in his life-time such fame abroad – his example and his invigorating, benevolent, commonsense presence have combined to give British sculptors an enhanced assurance and created an environment in which talent may flourish.

Moore is an inspiring rather than a didactic figure, and there is no clearer evidence of the fruitfulness of his influence than the relative absence, in the work of his younger contemporaries, of imitation of his own. Some, of course, there has been; but even among those who like Bernard Meadows (who works in Moore's studio from time to time) have had close personal contact with him, imitation has quickly receded as they have evolved personal styles. Before I refer to Moore's juniors, however, special note should be taken of the work of Barbara Hepworth, a member of his own generation. Her sculpture bears a resemblance to Moore's: both are in the main massive, immobile, austere and sharply defined. She has looked long and carefully at the early sculpture from which he drew much of his inspiration; nor has she neglected to keep a sharp eye upon what he has been about. Yet even when to a superficial glance their work has seemed closest, it is in fact the emanation of temperaments which have little in common. Although like him she is an artist obsessed by a few relatively simple ideas, she inclines to treat them differently. He develops them slowly, feeling his way towards extensions, sometimes remote extensions of them, sometimes, unusually confident though he is, with hesitation, bred of doubt but tending always towards a larger humanity expressed in ampler and more eloquent forms. She is more concerned to perfect than to evolve, and where she does evolve it is by a logical progression from point to point. In this age, when the abstract tide is running strongly, many artists adopt abstract modes of expression unsuited to their innermost needs. Not so Barbara Hepworth: like Ben Nicholson she speaks the language of abstraction with entire naturalness, and with the purest accent. She speaks it thus because it is the language of her thought. How clearly she understands the primal condition of true abstract art and the working of her own mind is evident from the following quotation from one of her writings: 'The understanding of form and colour in the abstract is an essential of carving or painting; but it is not simply the desire to avoid naturalism in the carving that leads to an abstract work. I feel that the conception itself, the quality of the thought that is embodied, must be abstract – an impersonal vision individualised in the particular medium.'[1] The more abstract her work, the freer from any resemblance to anything in the visible world, the more truly does it reflect the mind, clear-cut, uncompromising and wholly assured, of Barbara Hepworth.

1. Catalogue of retrospective exhibition 1927–1954, at the Whitechapel Art Gallery, 1954, p. 13.

DURING the years which have followed the ending of the Second World War a new generation of sculptors has emerged in Britain who have quickly won respectful attention at home and resounding success abroad. If the climate of confidence, the readiness to tread untrodden ways, was largely the creation of Moore, the work of this emerging generation owes more to Picasso, to Giacometti, and even to Calder than it does to Moore. Most conspicuously their sculpture differs from his in the matter of sheer bulk. The sculpture of Moore is massive (there is a suggestion of massiveness in his smallest figures), and it is serene. The sculpture of these emerging figures very rarely exhibits either characteristic. Instead it is commonly wiry and nervous. 'They have seized Eliot's image of the Hollow Men,' wrote Herbert Read (in the Introduction to catalogue of British Council Touring Exhibition 'Young British Sculptors', 1955–56) 'they have peopled the Waste Land with their iron waifs.' They have these and other characteristics in common – metal, often forged iron, as their chosen material, and the avoidance, in the main, of anything approaching a close representation of nature – but in no sense do they form a group and their aims are distinct, even divergent. At most they are stimulated by one another's example, by their awareness that the art of sculpture is being pursued in their time and country with energy and imagination, and accorded a degree of recognition only accorded, as a rule and then only grudgingly, to the work of a very few of the eminent aged.

Among the most gifted of this new generation are Reg. Butler, Lynn Chadwick, F. E. McWilliam, Elisabeth Frink, Bernard Meadows, Ivor Roberts-Jones, Kenneth Armitage and Eduardo Paolozzi, and a recruit from painting, Michael Ayrton. Nor is there any sign of any slackening of the creative energy among British sculptors, for already members of a still younger generation have made their contribution to this spirited and adventurous renaissance. At the time of writing these words these sculptors of varied gifts are moving so rapidly in their exploration of new forms of plastic expression that it would seem premature to attempt an estimate of the achievement of any of them. However this renaissance will develop no one can tell, but in the meanwhile, for the first time since the Middle Ages, sculpture is being pursued in Britain with the same originality and vigour as painting; if indeed some intelligent foreign observers are right, with a larger measure of both.

PLATES

PLATES

THE PAINTINGS, DRAWINGS AND SCULPTURES illustrated on the following plates are owned by the private collectors and public galleries or authorities listed below. Grateful acknowledgement is made to the artists or their executors and to the owners for permitting the reproductions and for supplying photographs and information.

H.M. Queen Elizabeth the Queen Mother, 73
Sir Robert Adeane, 47
Mr. Thomas Adler, 153
Sir Colin Anderson, 120, 148
Mr. Albert L. Arenberg, 143
Michael Ayrton, Esq., 131
The Hon. Robert Baring, 104
Executors of the late Geoffrey Blackwell, 7
Howard Bliss, Esq., 123
Mrs. Mary Bone, 89
Ralph Brown, Esq., 129
L. J. Cadbury, Esq., 80, 81
Lady Mary Campbell, 31
H. G. Carr, Esq., 56
Sir Kenneth Clark, 44
Sir William Coldstream, 68
The Countess of Crawford and Balcarres, 3
Roy de Maistre, Esq., 109
Dr. Harold Fletcher, 106
Brinsley Ford, Esq., 97
Mrs. Peggy Guggenheim, 147
F. W. Halliday, Esq., 45
Martin Halperin, Esq., 1
Col. Robert D. Q. Henriques, 32
Jeremy Hutchinson, Esq., 86
M. Nesto Jacometti, 155
Mr. Edgar Jones, 113
Major E. O. Kay, 78
R. N. Kershaw, Esq., 150
W. J. Keswick, Esq., 116
Mr. Oskar Klein, 103
R. A. B. Mynors, Esq., 87
Mrs. Cynthia Nolan, 121
John Piper, Esq., 17
The Hon. Mrs. Arthur Pollen, 26
T. H. Priestley, Esq., 30

The Hon. Mrs. Rayner, 111
C. S. Reddihough, Esq., 134
The Hon. Richard and Mrs. Rhys, 82, 108
Ceri Richards, Esq., 141
Mr. and Mrs. John Rood, 118
Sir John Rothenstein, 18, 57, 58, 122
Michael Rothenstein, Esq., 152
J. D. Sainsbury, Esq., 125
Executors of the late Morton Sands, 4
Mrs. Violet Schiff, 34
Sir Selwyn Selwyn-Clarke, 124
Gordon Small, Esq., 107
Jack Smith, Esq., 102
Mrs. Graham Sutherland, 119
Miss Helen Sutherland, 135
Mrs. Dudley Tooth, 28
Mrs. Julian Vinogradoff, 27
Mrs. Lucy Carrington Wertheim, 98
James Wood, Esq., 91
S. John Woods, Esq., 76
Sir William Worsley, Bt., 75
The Hon. Mrs. Henry Yorke, 65

*   *

Aberdeen Art Gallery, 6, 72
Batley, Bagshaw Art Gallery, 132
Birmingham City Art Gallery, 2, 51
Brighton Art Gallery, 21
Buffalo, Albright Art Gallery, 154
Burghclere, Oratory of All Souls, 88
Cambridge, Jesus College, 145
Cardiff, National Museum of Wales, 15
Chicago Art Institute, 133
Durban Museum and City Art Gallery, 74
Glasgow Art Gallery, 50

Kingston-upon-Hull, Ferens Art Gallery, 38
Leeds City Art Gallery, 84, 101
Leicestershire County Council, 112
Liverpool, Walker Art Gallery, 99
London
  Arts Council of Great Britain, 151
  Ben Uri Gallery, 85
  Bethnal Green Borough Council, 127
  British Council, 20, 46, 95
  Convent of the Holy Child Jesus, 40
  Hanover Gallery, 138
  Imperial War Museum, 41, 126
  Lefevre Gallery, 83
  Marlborough Gallery, 71
  Tate Gallery, 8, 9, 10, 11, 12, 13, 14, 16, 22, 24, 25, 33, 35, 36, 37, 39, 42, 43, 48, 49, 52, 54, 55, 59, 61, 63, 64, 67, 70, 79, 90, 92, 93, 94, 100, 105, 110, 114, 115, 128, 130, 137, 139, 140, 149
  University College, 62
Londonderry, Altnagelvin Hospital, 142
Manchester City Art Gallery, 19, 23, 69
Melbourne, National Gallery of Victoria, 29
New York, Museum of Modern Art, 136, 144, 146
Ottawa, National Gallery of Canada, 53
Oxford, Ashmolean Museum, 5
  Balliol College Junior Common Room, 77
  Campion Hall, 60
Sydney, National Gallery of New South Wales, 66, 117

1. W. R. Sickert: *The Lady in the Gondola*. Oil, 1905–1906. London, Coll. Martin Halperin, Esq.

2. W. R. Sickert: *St. Jacques, Dieppe*. Oil, 1900. Birmingham City Art Gallery

3. W. R. Sickert: *The Horses of St. Mark's*. Oil, 1901. Colinsburgh, Coll. The Countess of Crawford and Balcarres

4. W. R. Sickert: *The Baby Grand*. Pencil and black chalk, about 1914. London, Executors of the late Morton Sands, Esq.

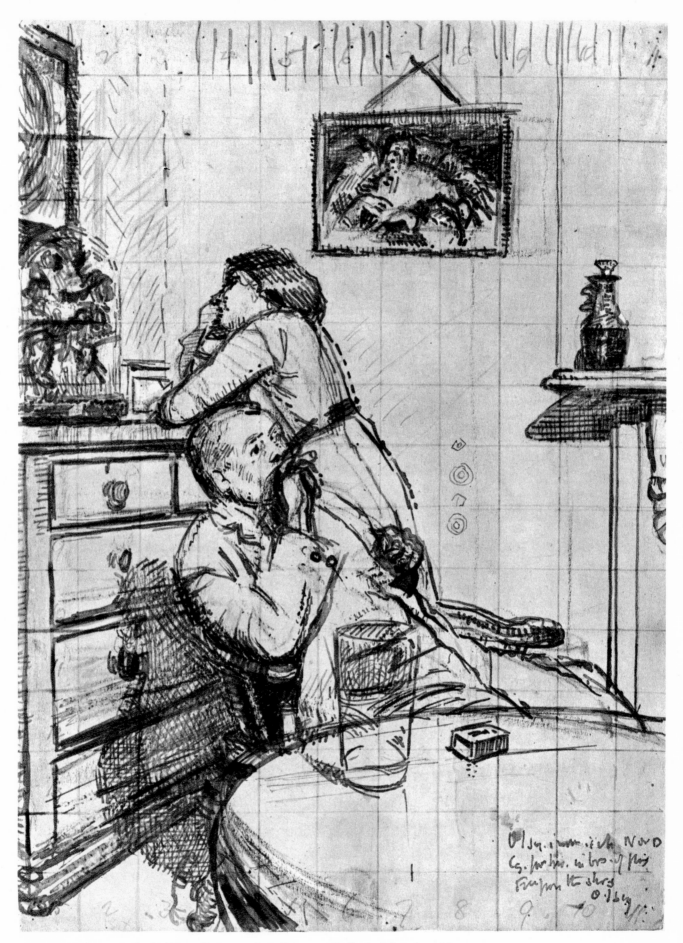

5. W. R. Sickert: *Study for "Ennui"*. Pen and chalk, 1913. Oxford, Ashmolean Museum

6. Wilson Steer: *The Horseshoe Bend of the Severn*. Oil, 1909. Aberdeen Art Gallery

7. Wilson Steer: *The Home Farm*. Oil, 1901. London, Executors of the late Geoffrey Blackwell, Esq.

8. Wilson Steer: *Mrs. Raynes*. Oil, 1922. London, Tate Gallery

9. Lucien Pissarro: *Ivy Cottage, Coldharbour*. Oil, 1916. London, Tate Gallery

10. Jack B. Yeats: *The Two Travellers*. Oil, 1942. London, Tate Gallery

11. Frances Hodgkins: *Broken Tractor*. Gouache, about 1942. London, Tate Gallery

12. William Nicholson: *Silver*. Oil, 1938. London, Tate Gallery

14. Spencer Gore: *North London Girl*. Oil, 1911. London, Tate Gallery

13. Ethel Walker: *Vanessa*. Oil, 1937. London, Tate Gallery

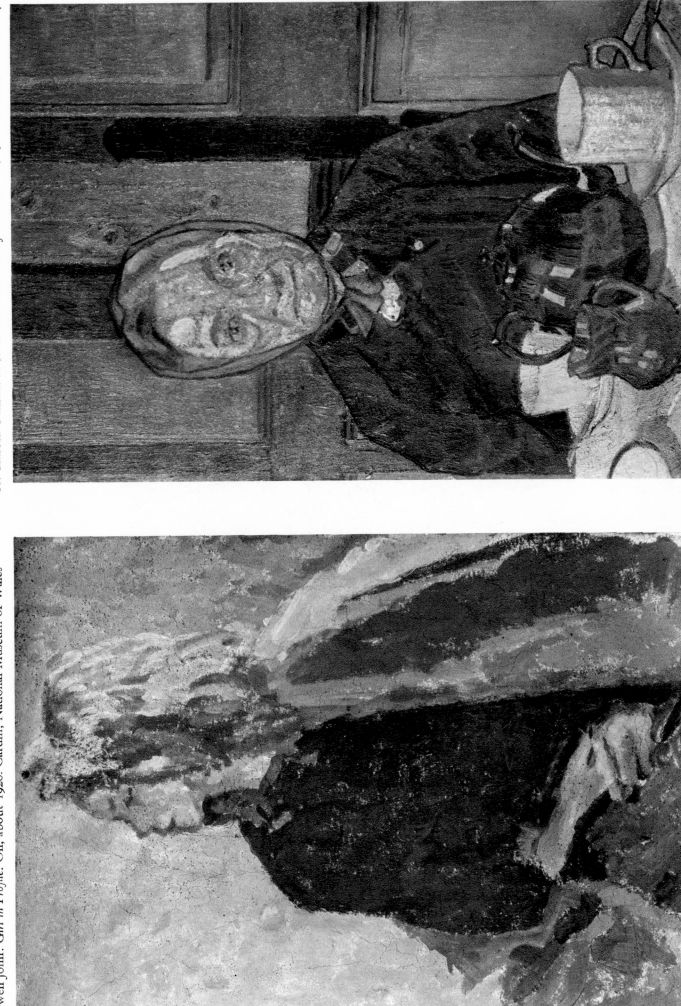

16. Harold Gilman: *Mrs. Mounter at the Breakfast Table*. Oil, 1916. London, Tate Gallery

15. Gwen John: *Girl in Profile*. Oil, about 1920. Cardiff, National Museum of Wales

17. Harold Gilman: *Oak Tree*. Pen drawing, about 1916. Henley, Coll. John Piper, Esq.

18. William Rothenstein: *Blasted Trees, Western Front*. Oil, 1918. Newington, Coll. Sir John Rothenstein

19. William Rothenstein: *The Church of St. Seine l'Abbaye*. Oil, 1906. Manchester City Art Gallery

20. Charles Ginner: *Aqueduct, Bath*. Oil, 1928.
Coll. British Council

21. Robert Bevan: *The Cabyard at Night*.
Oil, 1910. Brighton Art Gallery

22. Charles Ginner: *The Café Royal*. Oil, 1911. London, Tate Gallery

23. William Orpen: *Hommage à Manet*. Oil, 1910. Manchester City Art Gallery

24. Edward Ardizzone: *Priest begging for a Lift, Louvain, May 1940.* Pen and ink and watercolour. London, Tate Gallery

25. Henry Tonks: *Sodales – Mr. Steer and Mr. Sickert*. Oil, 1930. London, Tate Gallery

26. Ambrose McEvoy: *The Hon. Daphne Baring*. Oil, 1916. London, Coll. The Hon. Mrs. Arthur Pollen

27. Augustus John: *Lady Ottoline Morrell*. Oil, 1926. London, Coll. Mrs. Julian Vinogradoff

28. Augustus John: *Dorelia in Eastern Dr*
Watercolour, about 1906. London,
Coll. Mrs. Dudley Tooth

29. Augustus John: *His Honour H. C. Dowdall, K.C., as Lord Mayor of Liverpool*. Oil, 1908–1909. Melbourne, National Gallery of Victoria

30. Augustus John: *Two Children*. Pencil drawing, about 1900–1908. London, Coll. T. H. Priestley, Esq.

31. Augustus John: *Daphne*. Oil, 1937. Great Bedwin, Coll. Lady Mary Campbell

32. Augustus John: *Portrait Head of a Woman*. Charcoal drawing, about 1904. Cirencester, Coll. Col. Robert D. Q. Henriques

33. Henri Gaudier-Brzeska: *Sophie Brzeska*. Pastel, 1913. London, Tate Gallery

34. Henri Gaudier-Brzeska: *The Dancer*. Bronze, 1913.
London, Coll. Mrs. Violet Schiff

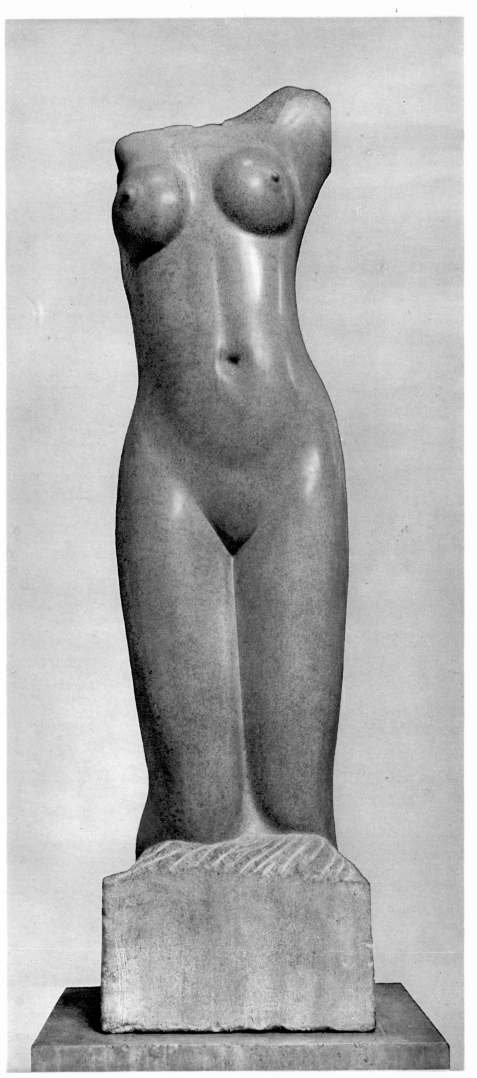

35. Eric Gill: *Mankind*:
Hoptonwood stone, 1927–1928.
London, Tate Gallery

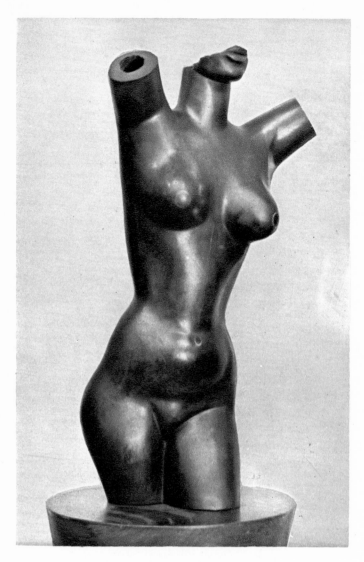

36. Leon Underwood: *Torso: The June of Youth*. Bronze, 1937. London, **Tate Gallery**

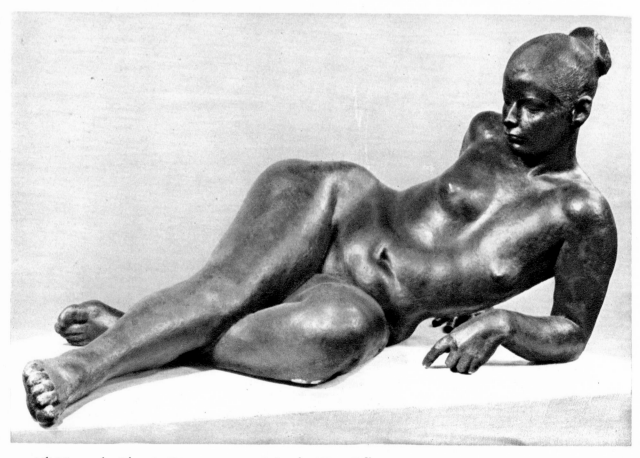

37. Uli Nimptsch: *Olympia*. Bronze, 1953–1956. London, Tate Gallery

38. Jacob Epstein: *Isobel*. Bronze, 1931. Kingston-upon-Hull, Ferens Art Gallery

39. Jacob Epstein: *The Rock Drill*. Bronze, 1913. London, Tate Gallery

40. Jacob Epstein: *Madonna and Child*. Lead, 1951. London, Convent of the Holy Child Jesus, Cavendish Square

41. Jacob Epstein: *Admiral of the Fleet Lord Fisher of Kilverstone, G.C.B., O.M., G.C.V.O.* Bronze, 1915. London, Imperial War Museum

42. Eric Kennington: *Recumbent Figure of T. E. Lawrence* (detail). Ciment fondu, 1939–1954. London, Tate Gallery

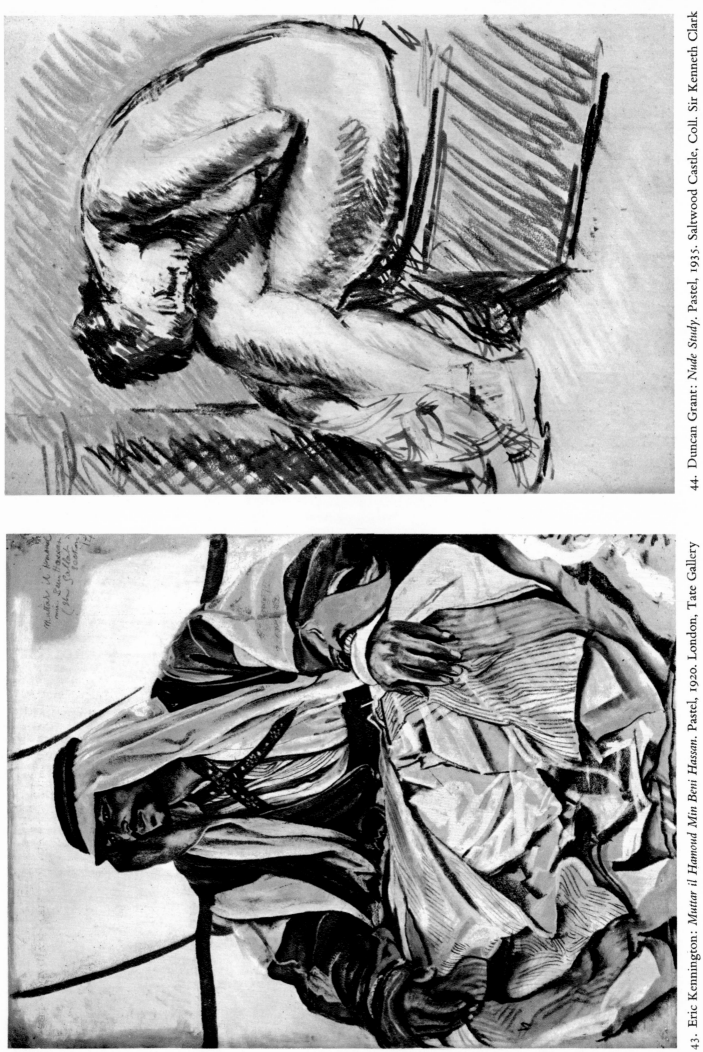

44. Duncan Grant: *Nude Study*. Pastel, 1935. Saltwood Castle, Coll. Sir Kenneth Clark

43. Eric Kennington: *Muttar il Hamoud Min Beni Hassan*. Pastel, 1920. London, Tate Gallery

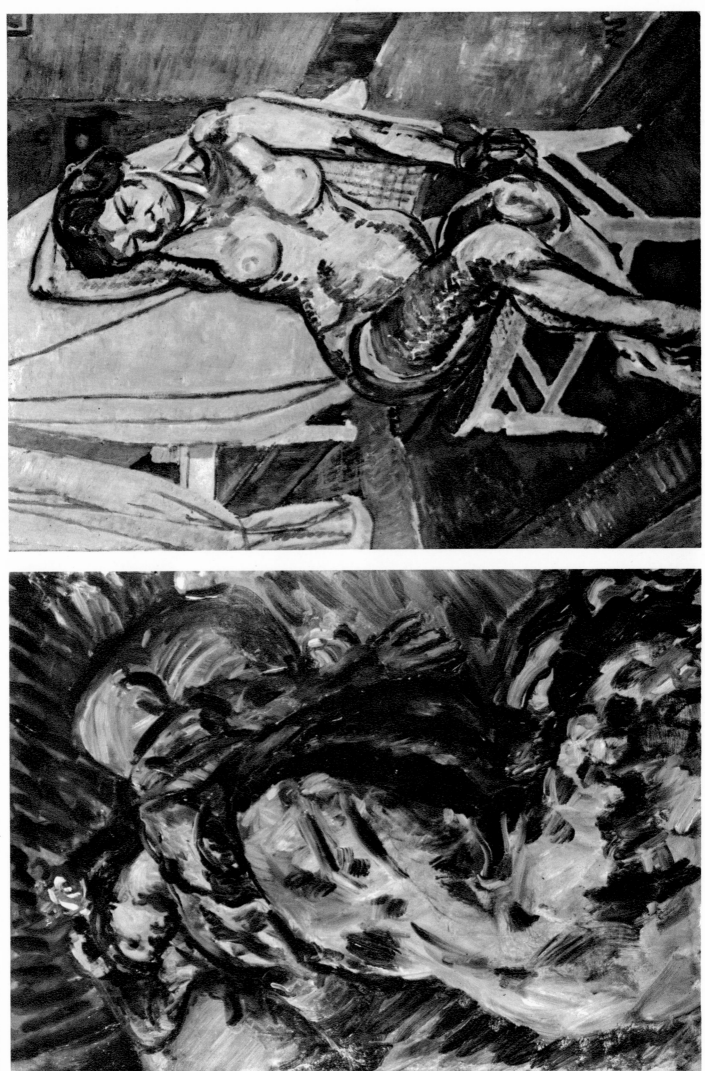

47. Matthew Smith: *Winter in Provence*. Oil, about 1937. London, Coll. Sir Robert Adeane

48. James Dickson Innes: *The Waterfall*. Watercolour, 1910. London, Tate Gallery

49. Vanessa Bell: *Flowers in a Jug*. Oil, 1920. London, Tate Gallery

50. L. S. Lowry: *River Scene*. Oil, 1942. Glasgow Art Gallery

51. John Nash: *Winter Afternoon*. Watercolour, 1945. Birmingham City Art Gallery

52. Anthony Gross: *Gateway into Germany – the Maas in Flood near the Berg Bridge*. Watercolour, 1944. London, Tate Gallery

53. Victor Pasmore: *Evening – Hammersmith*. Oil, 1943. Ottawa, National Gallery of Canada

54. William Townsend: *Hop Alleys*. Oil, 1951–1952.
London, Tate Gallery

55. W. G. Gillies: *Esperston*. Oil, 1950. London, Tate Gallery

56. Edward Bawden: *Ives' Farm*. Oil, 1954. Cambridge, Coll. H. G. Carr, Esq.

57. Albert Houthuesen: *Trees in Ruskin Park*. Chalk drawing, 1960. Newington, Coll. Sir John Rothenstein

58. Albert Houthuesen: *The Supper at Emmaus*. Oil, 1927–1928. Newington, Coll. Sir John Rothenstein

59. Edward Le Bas: *Interior*. Oil, 1951. London, Tate Gallery

60. Charles Mahoney: *The Nativity*. Oil, about 1950. Oxford, Campion Hall

61. Rodrigo Moynihan: *The Teaching Staff of the Royal College of Art*. Oil, 1951. London, Tate Gallery

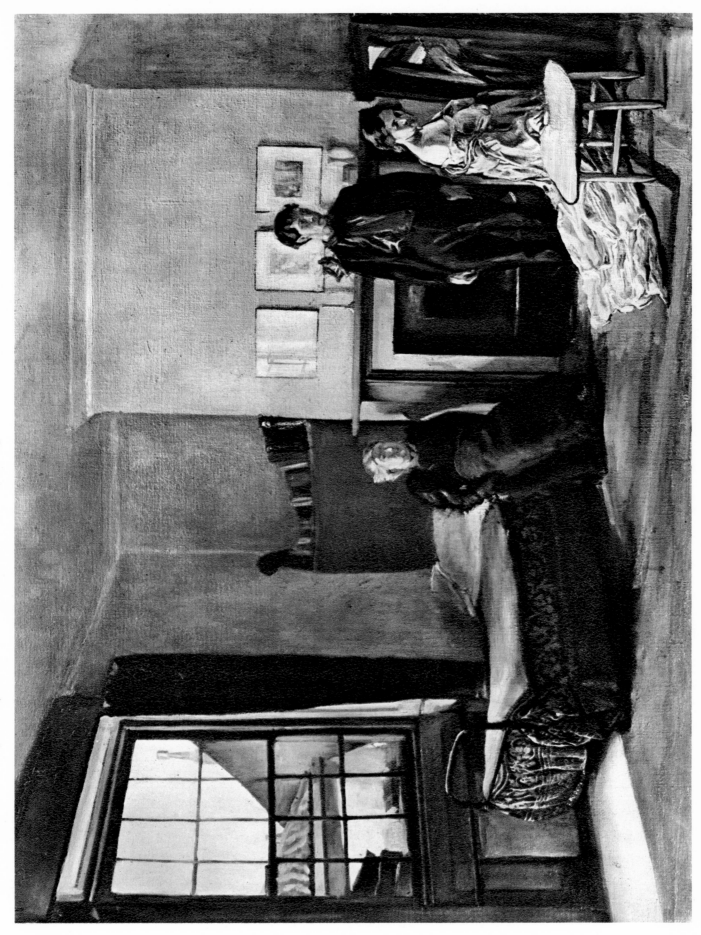

62. Albert Rutherston: *The Confessions of Claude.* Oil, 1901. London, University College

63. Duncan Grant: *Vanessa Bell*. Oil, 1942. London, Tate Gallery

64. Henry Lamb: *Lytton Strachey*. Oil, 1914. London, Tate Gallery

65. Lawrence Gowing: *Lady Asleep*. Oil, 1945. London, Coll. The Hon. Mrs. Henry Yorke

66. Allan Gwynne-Jones: *Miss Diana Hunt*. Oil, 1944. Sydney, National Gallery of New South Wales

67. William Coldstream: *Mrs. S. G. H. Burger*. Oil, 1936–1937. London, Tate Gallery

68. William Coldstream: *The Studio*. Oil, 1932–1933. In the artist's possession

69. Wyndham Lewis: *Portrait of a Girl Standing.*
Chalk drawing, 1920.
Manchester City Art Gallery

Wyndham Lewis: *Edith Sitwell*. Oil, 1923–1935. London, Tate Gallery

71. Wyndham Lewis: *Revolution*. Oil, about 1917. London, **Marlborough Gallery**

72. Paul Nash: *Northern Adventure*. Oil, 1929. Aberdeen Art Gallery

73. Paul Nash: *Landscape of the Vernal Equinox*. Oil, 1943. Coll. **H.M. Queen Elizabeth the Queen Mother**

74. Paul Nash: *Monster Field*. Oil, 1939. Durban Art Gallery

75. John Piper: *Hovingham Hall, Yorkshire*. Watercolour, 1944. Hovingham Hall, Coll. Sir William Worsley, Bt.

76. John Piper: *Monument at Waldershare*. Watercolour, 1947. London, Coll. S. John Woods, Esq.

77. Derrick Greaves: *Sheffield*. Oil, 1953. Oxford, Balliol College Junior Common Room

78. Tristram Hillier: *Viseu*. Oil, 1947. Hove, Coll. Major E. O. Kay

79. John Minton: *Street and Railway Bridge*. Oil, 1946. London, Tate Gallery

80. C. R. W. Nevinson: *Column on the March*. Oil, 1915. Birmingham, Coll. L. J. Cadbury, Esq.

81. C. R. W. Nevinson: *La Patrie*. Oil, 1916. Birmingham, Coll. L. J. Cadbury, Esq.

82. Edward Burra: *John Deth*. Gouache, 1932. London, Coll. The Hon. Richard and Mrs. Rhys

83. Edward Burra: *Elephant Lady*. Watercolour, 1955. London, Lefevre Gallery

84. David Bomberg: *Jewish Theatre (The Pavilion, Whitechapel)*. Black chalk, 1913. Leeds City Art Gallery

85. Mark Gertler: *Roundabout*. Oil, 1916. London, Ben Uri Gallery

86. Mark Gertler: *Rabbi and Rabbitzen*. Oil, 1914. London, Coll. Jeremy Hutchinson, Esq.

7. Stanley Spencer: *Beatitudes of Love. II, Knowing*. Oil, 1938. Oxford, Coll. R. A. B. Mynors, Esq.

89. Stanley Spencer: *Zacharias and Elizabeth*. Oil, 1912–1913. London, Coll. Mrs. Mary Bone

88 (opposite). Stanley Spencer: *Resurrection, Salonika Front*. Oil, 1928–1929. Burghclere, Oratory of All Souls

90. Stanley Spencer: *Joachim among the Shepherds*. Pen and wash, 1912.

London, Tate Gallery

91. Stanley Spencer: *The Visitation*. Oil, 1913. London, Coll. James Wood, Esq.

92. Stanley Spencer: *Self-Portrait*. Oil, 1913. London, Tate Gallery

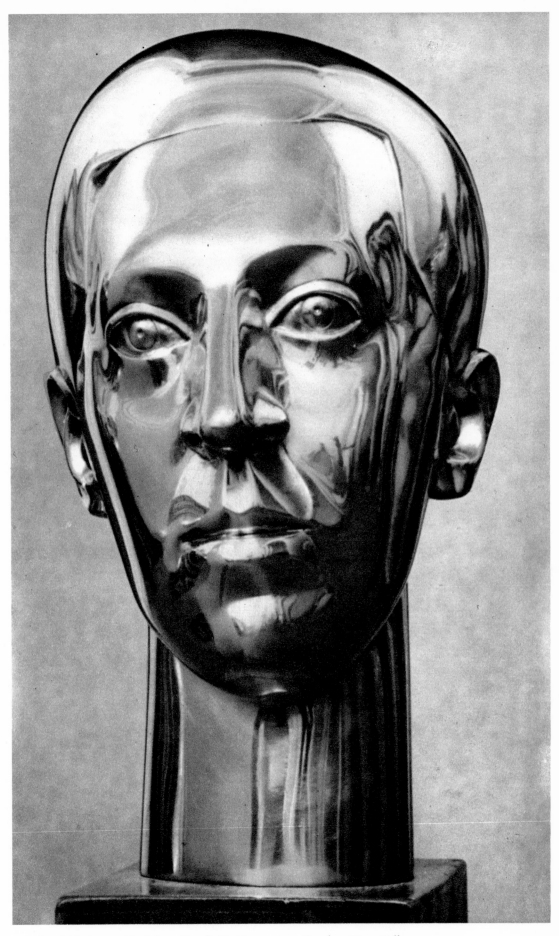

93. Frank Dobson: *Sir Osbert Sitwell, Bt.* Brass, 1923. London, Tate Gallery

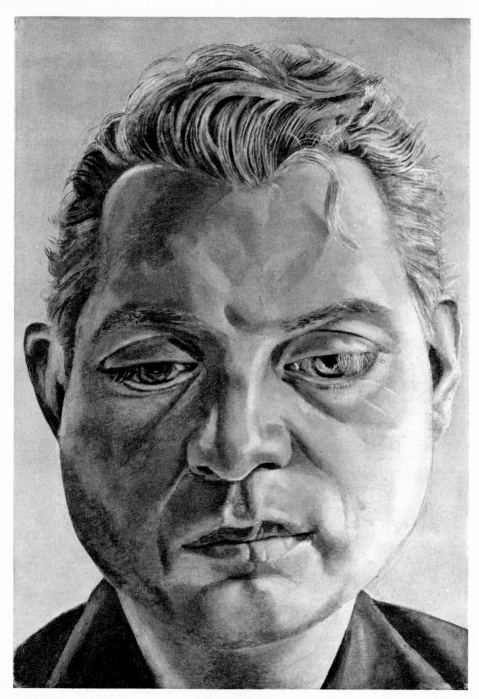

94. Lucian Freud: *Francis Bacon*. Oil, 1952. London, Tate Gallery

95. Lucian Freud: *Girl with a Rose*. Oil, 1947–1948. Coll. British Council

96. David Jones: *Aphrodite in Aulis*. Pen and watercolour, 1941. Private Coll.

97. Christopher Wood: *The Yellow Man*. 1930. London, Coll. Brinsley Ford, Esq.

98. Christopher Wood: *The Yellow Horse*. Oil, 1930. Brighton, Coll. Mrs. Lucy Carrington Wertheim

99. Jack Smith: *Creation and Crucifixion*. Oil, 1956. Liverpool, Walker Art Gallery

100. Claude Rogers: *The Blowlamp*. Oil, 1954. London, Tate Gallery

101. Edward Wadsworth: *Marine*. Tempera, 1928. Leeds City Art Gallery

102. Jack Smith: *Waves of Light over Glasses*. Oil, 1958. In the artist's possession

103. John Bratby: *Shovelton, Bailley, Lessore, Sandford, Bratby, Innes*. Oil, 1957. New York, Coll. Mr. Oskar Klein

104. Cecil Collins: *Christ before the Judge*. Oil, 1954. London, Coll. The Hon. Robert Baring

105. Cecil Collins: *The Sleeping Fool*. Oil, 1943. London, Tate Gallery

106. John Maxwell: *Landscape with Dead Trees*. Watercolour, 1947. Edinburgh, Coll. Dr. Harold Fletcher

107. John Maxwell: *Woman with Flowers*. Oil, 1941. Edinburgh, Coll. Gordon Small, Esq.

108. Roy de Maistre: *Noli me tangere*. Oil, about 1951. London, Coll. The Hon. Richard and Mrs. Rhys

109. Roy de Maistre: *Veiled Madonna*. Oil, 1946. In the artist's possession

110. John Craxton: *Hotel by the Sea*. Oil, 1946. London, Tate Gallery

111. Robin Ironside: *Visitor to a Museum Posing on a Vacant Plinth*. Watercolour, 1955. London, Coll. The Hon. Mrs. Rayner

112. Edward Middleditch: *Pigeons in Trafalgar Square*. Oil, 1954. Leicestershire County Council

113. Josef Herman: *Two Miners*. Pastel, 1945. Washington, Coll. Mr. Edgar Jones

114. Henry Moore: *Pink and Green Sleepers*. Wash and crayon, 1941. London, Tate Gallery

115. Henry Moore: *Two-piece Reclining Figure No. 2*. Bronze, 1960. London, Tate Gallery

116 (opposite). Henry Moore: *King and Queen*. Bronze, 1952–1953. Shawhead, Coll. W. J. Keswick, Esq.

117. Henry Moore: *Helmet Head No. 2*. Bronze, 1950. Sydney, National Gallery of New South Wales

118. Barbara Hepworth: *Two Figures*. Wood with white paint, 1947–1948. Minneapolis, Coll. Mr. and Mrs. John Rood

119. Graham Sutherland: *Three Standing Forms in a Garden*, II. Oil, 1952. Collection Mrs. Graham Sutherland

120. Graham Sutherland: *Blasted Oak*. Pen and wash, 1941. London, Coll. Sir Colin Anderson

121. Sidney Nolan: *Ram caught in a Flood*. Ripolin on masonite, 1955. London, Coll. Mrs. Cynthia Nolan

122. **Alan** Reynolds: *Upright Design*. Gouache, 1956. Newington, Coll. Sir John Rothenstein

123. Ivon Hitchens: *Millpool, Coming Storm.* Oil, 1951. London, Coll. Howard Bliss, Esq.

124. Ivon Hitchens: *Waterfall, Terwick Mill*. Oil, 1945. London, Coll. Sir Selwyn Selwyn-Clarke, K.B.E., C.M.G., M.C., M.D.

125. Anthony Fry: *Dancing Figures No. 3*. Oil, 1958. London, Coll. J. D. Sainsbury, Esq.

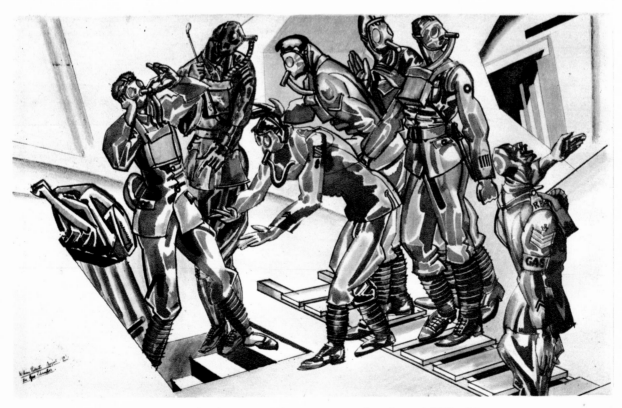

126. William Roberts: *The Gas Chamber*. Watercolour, 1918. London, Imperial War Museum

27. Elisabeth Frink: *Blind Man and Dog*. Bronze, 1958. Bethnal Green Borough Council

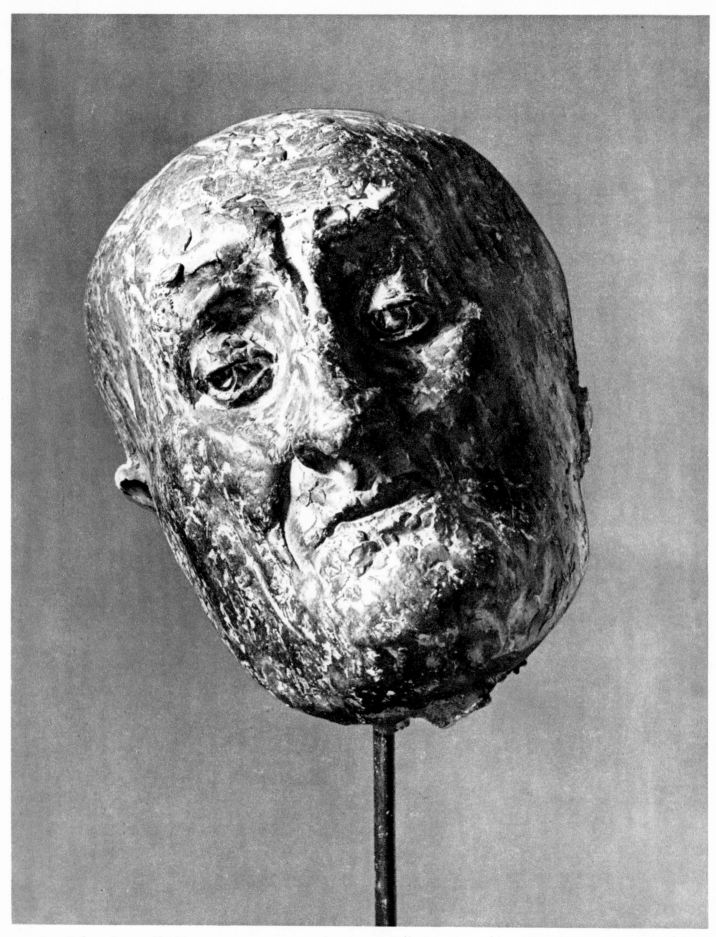

128. Ivor Roberts-Jones: *Claudel*. Bronze, 1956–1959. London, Tate Gallery

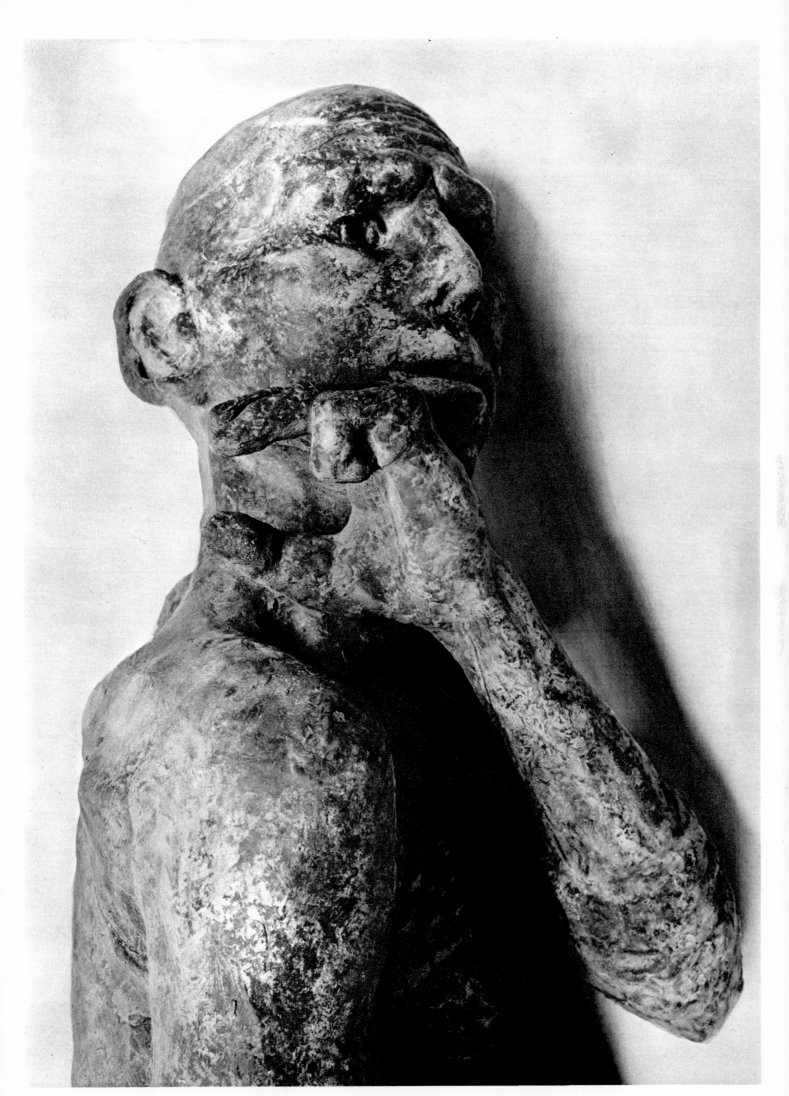

129. Ralph Brown: *Clochard* (Detail.) Concrete, 1955. In the artist's possession

130. Reg Butler: *Girl*.
Bronze, 1953–1954.
London, Tate Gallery

131. Michael Ayrton: *Mother and Child Bathing.*
Bronze, 1956–1957. In the artist's possession

132. Francis Bacon: *The Magdalen*. Oil, 1946. Batley, Bagshaw Art Gallery

133. Francis Bacon: *Head surrounded by Sides of Beef.* Oil, 1954. Chicago, Art Institute

134. Ben Nicholson: *St. Ives, 1940*. Oil on board. Ilkley, Coll. C. S. Reddihough, Esq.

135. Ben Nicholson: *Porthmeor, St. Ives, 1928*. Oil. Penrith, Coll. Miss Helen Sutherland

136. Ben Nicholson: *Painted Relief 1939 (version 1)*. Oil. New York, Museum of Modern Art

137. William Scott: *Winter Still Life*. Oil, 1956. London, Tate Gallery

138. William Scott: *Nearing Circles*. Oil, 1961. London, Hanover Gallery

139. Victor Pasmore: *Linear Motif, Black and White*. Oil and gravure on formica, 1960–1961. London, Tate Gallery

140. Ceri Richards: *Two Females*. Wood collage, 1937. London, Tate Gallery

141. Ceri Richards: *Falling Forms*. Oil, 1944. In the artist's possession

142. F. E. McWilliam: *Princess Macha.* Bronze, 1957. Londonderry, Altnagelvin Hospital

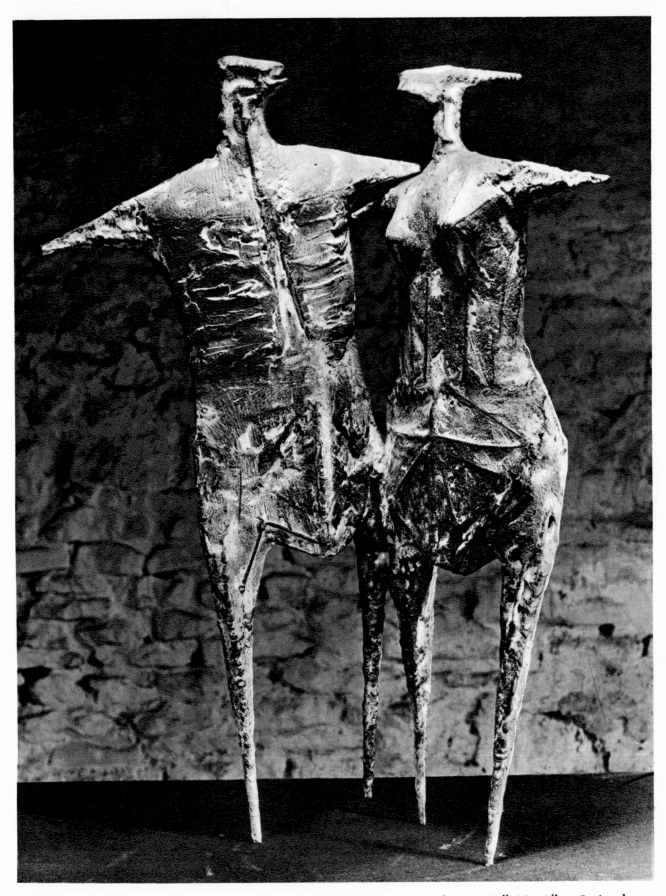

143. Lynn Chadwick: *Two Dancing Figures VI*. Iron and Composition, 1955. Chicago, Coll. Mr. Albert L. Arenberg

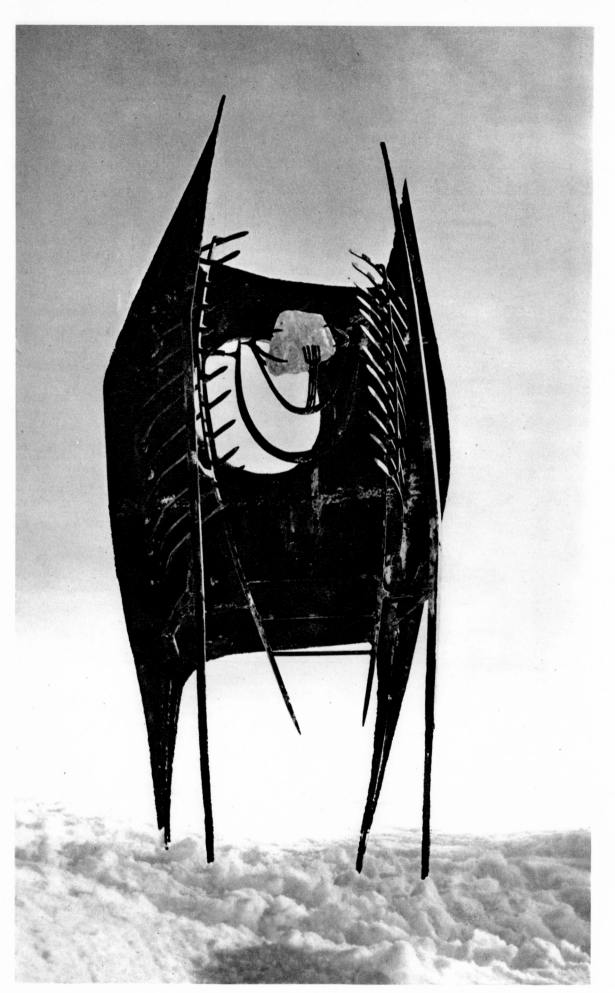

144. Lynn Chadwick: *The Inner Eye*. Iron and glass, 1952. New York, Museum of Modern Art

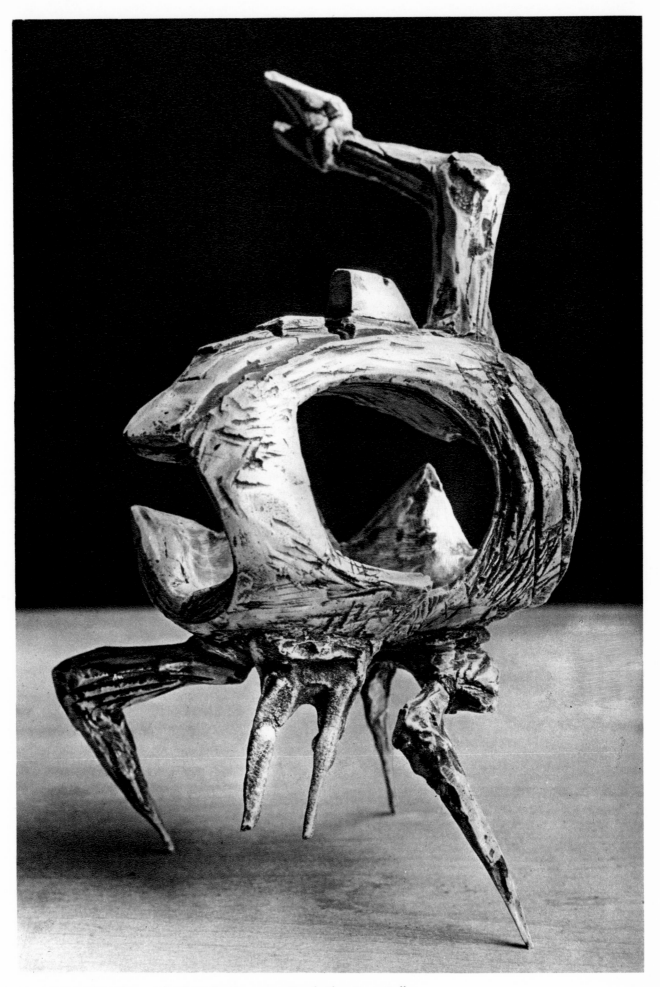

145. Bernard Meadows: *The Crab*. Bronze, 1954. Cambridge, Jesus College

146. Eduardo Paolozzi: *Jason 1956*. Bronze. New York, Museum of Modern Art

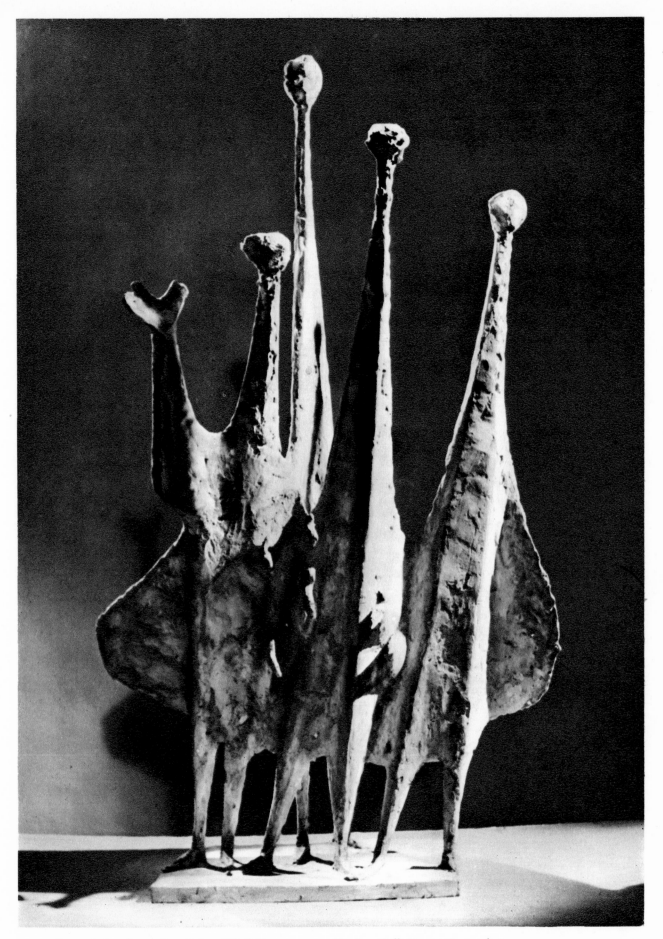

147. Kenneth Armitage: *People in a Wind*. Bronze, 1951. Venice, Coll. Peggy Guggenheim

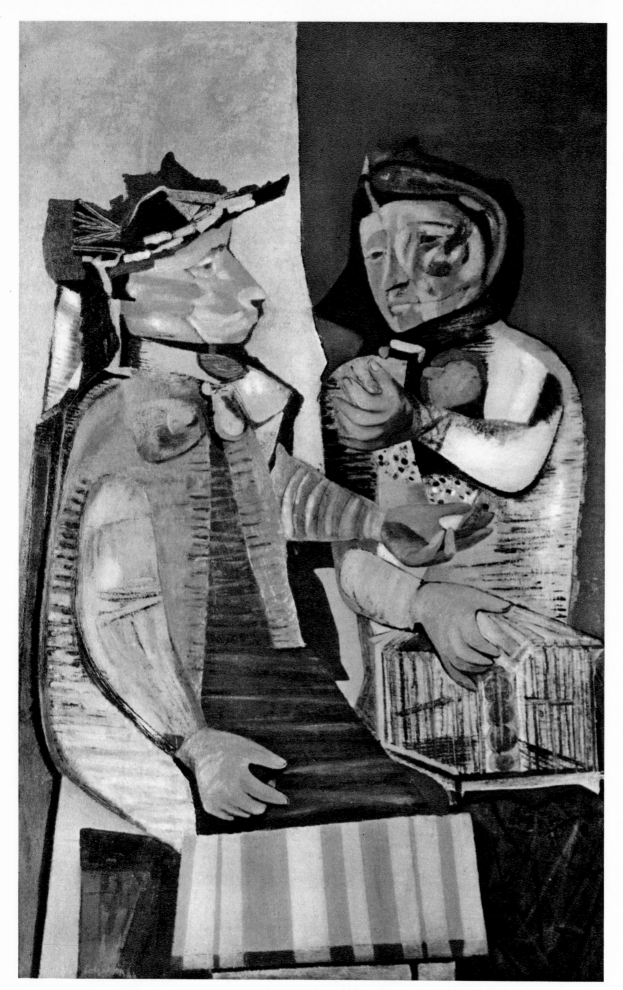

148. Robert Colquhoun: *The Fortune Teller*. Oil, 1946. London, Coll. Sir Colin Anderson

149. Robert McBryde: *Woman with Paper Flower*. Oil, 1944. London, Tate Gallery

150. Keith Vaughan: *Nude against a Rock*. Oil, 1957–1958. Wargrave, Coll. R. N. Kershaw, Esq.

151. Keith Vaughan: *The Village*. Oil, 1953. London, Arts Council of Great Britain

152. Michael Rothenstein: *Boat and Rocks*. Mixed media, 1958. In the artist's possession

153. Peter Lanyon: *Sand Bar*. Oil, 1956. Chicago, Coll. Thomas Adler

154. Alan Davie: *Male and Female*. Oil, 1955. Buffalo, Albright Art Gallery

155. Stanley William Hayter: *Labyrinth*. Oil, 1953.
Zurich, Coll. M. Nesto Jacometti

BIOGRAPHICAL NOTES ON THE ARTISTS
AND LIST OF ILLUSTRATIONS

NOTE

THE introductory text of this book was completed in the summer of 1957, and although in the proofs of it in 1961 I made a few minor corrections I thought it better to leave it unchanged. The brief biographies, however, have been brought up to date. Many of the artists represented in the present volume are discussed at greater length in my *Modern English Painters* (vol. I, 1952; vol. II, 1956).

May I make grateful acknowledgement to all owners of pictures and sculptures who have permitted their reproduction? I owe a special debt of gratitude to Miss Corinne Bellow, who has given many hours of her leisure time to the transcription of a difficult manuscript and to the checking of much information, a task in which she was assisted by Miss Odette Salway, to whom also my thanks are due.

1962   J.R.

BIOGRAPHICAL NOTES ON THE ARTISTS
AND LIST OF ILLUSTRATIONS

Edward ARDIZZONE

Born 1900 in Haiphong, Tonkin, China. Brought to England at the age of five. Studied at the Westminster School of Art and at the Central School of Arts and Crafts. First one-man exhibition in London in 1931. Official Artist in World War II. Has illustrated many books.

Priest begging for a Lift, Louvain. May 1940. Pen and ink and watercolour, 9½×12⅛ in. Tate Gallery, London. [Plate 24]

Kenneth ARMITAGE

Born 1916 in Leeds. Studied at the Slade School. Served in World War II. First one-man exhibition in London in 1952. Taught at the Bath Academy of Art. Gregory Fellow at Leeds University. Awarded David E. Bright Prize when his sculpture was shown in the British Pavilion at the Venice Biennale in 1958. A retrospective exhibition held at the Whitechapel Art Gallery in 1959.

People in a Wind. 1951. Bronze, 25½ in. high. Coll. Mrs. Peggy Guggenheim, Venice. [Plate 147]

Michael AYRTON

Born 1921 in London. Studied at Heatherley's, the St. John's Wood School of Art, and in Paris. First one-man exhibition in London in 1943. Has designed for the theatre and ballet, illustrated a number of books and written art criticism.

Mother and Child Bathing. 1956-7. Bronze, 38 in. high. In the artist's possession. [Plate 131]

Francis BACON

Born 1909 in Dublin but lives in London. Began to paint in the early 1930's. Self-taught. First one-man exhibition in London in 1949, in New York in 1953 and in Paris in 1957. Represented in the British Pavilion at the Venice Biennale in 1954. Made several prolonged visits to North Africa.

Study for the Magdalen. 1946. Oil, 55×49 in. Bagshaw Art Gallery, Batley. [Plate 132]
Head surrounded by Sides of Beef. 1954. Oil, 60×46 in. Art Institute of Chicago. [Plate 133]

Edward BAWDEN

Born 1903 in Braintree, Essex. Studied at the Cambridge School of Art and the Royal College of Art. First one-man exhibition in London in 1934. Carried out several wall-paintings; has also designed for the theatre and for industry,

and has illustrated books. Official Artist in World War II. Taught at the Royal College of Art. Trustee of the Tate Tallery.

Lit.: *Edward Bawden* (Penguin Modern Painters), by J. M. Richards, 1946.

Ives' Farm. 1954. Oil, 22½×18 in. Coll. Hugh G. Carr, Esq., Cambridge. [Plate 56]

Vanessa BELL

Born 1879 in London; sister of Virginia Woolf. Studied at the Royal Academy Schools. Married the art critic Clive Bell. Associated with Roger Fry in the Omega Workshops, and with Duncan Grant in several schemes of wall decoration. Died 1961. A memorial exhibition held in London in 1961.

Flowers in a Jug. 1920. Oil, 24×18 in. Tate Gallery, London. [Plate 49]

Robert BEVAN

Born 1865 in Hove, Sussex. Studied at the Westminster School and at the Académie Julian, Paris. Spent 1893-94 at Pont Aven, where he met Gauguin. An original member of the Camden Town Group and of the London Group. First one-man exhibition in London in 1905. Died 1925. Memorial exhibitions held in London and the Brighton Art Gallery in 1926, and a retrospective exhibition at the Arts Council Gallery in 1956.

The Cabyard at Night. 1910. Oil, 24×27 in. Brighton Art Gallery. [Plate 21]

David BOMBERG

Born 1890 in Birmingham. Studied at the City and Guilds School and attended evening classes at Westminster School under Sickert. First one-man exhibition in London in 1914. Foundation member of the London Group. Served in World War I. Formed the Borough Group in 1947 and the Borough Bottega in 1953. Lived largely in Spain during his last years and died in London in 1957. Retrospective exhibitions held at the Arts Council Gallery in 1958, and in Coventry in 1960.

Jewish Theatre (The Pavilion, Whitechapel). 1913. Black chalk, 21¾×23¾ in. Leeds City Art Gallery. [Plate 84]

John BRATBY

Born 1928 in Wimbledon. Studied at the Kingston School of Art and at the Royal College of Art, where he won scholarships which enabled him to visit Italy. First one-man exhibition in London in 1954. Represented in the British Pavilion at the Venice Biennale in 1956. Won the British

Section Guggenheim Award for Painting in 1956 and jointly with Ben Nicholson in 1958. Novelist.

Shovelton, Bailley, Lessore, Sandford, Bratby, Innes. 1957. Oil, 120×77½ in. Coll. Mr. Oskar Klein, New York. [Plate 103]

Ralph BROWN

Born 1928 in Leeds. Studied at the Leeds College of Art, at the Royal College of Art, and in Paris with Zadkine in 1954. Travelled in Greece and Italy. Taught at the Royal College of Art. First one-man exhibition in London in 1961.

Clochard. 1955. Concrete, 60 in. long. In the artist's possession. [Plate 129]

Edward BURRA

Born 1905 in London. Studied at the Chelsea School of Art and the Royal College of Art. First one-man exhibition in London in 1929. Designed for ballet. Travelled in Spain, Mexico, U.S.A. and elsewhere. Exhibits infrequently.

Lit.: *Edward Burra* (Penguin Modern Painters), by Sir John Rothenstein, 1945.

John Deth. 1932. Gouache, 22×30 in. Coll. The Hon. Richard and Mrs. Rhys, London. [Plate 82]
Elephant Lady. 1955. Watercolour, 23×30½ in. Lefevre Gallery, London. [Plate 83]

Reginald BUTLER

Born 1913 in Buntingford, Hertfordshire. Trained as an architect. Gave up architecture for sculpture in 1945; about two years later helped Henry Moore in carving his *Three Figures* now in Battersea Park. First one-man exhibition in London in 1949 and in New York in 1953; represented in the British Pavilion at the Venice Biennale in 1952. Awarded First Prize in the International Sculpture Competition "The Unknown Political Prisoner" held at the Tate Gallery in 1953, where the model he submitted was destroyed by a protesting member of the public.

Girl. 1953–54. Shell bronze, 70 in. high. Tate Gallery, London. [Plate 130]

Lynn CHADWICK

Born 1914 in London. Trained as an architect. Following his war service he began in 1945 to make mobiles. First one-man exhibition in London in 1953. Awarded a prize in the "Unknown Political Prisoner" competition at the Tate Gallery in 1953, and the International Sculpture Prize when his work was shown in the British Pavilion at the Venice Biennale in 1956.

Lit.: *Lynn Chadwick*, by Sir Herbert Read (Amerswil), 1960. – *Chadwick*, by J. P. Hodin, 1961.

Two Dancing Figures. VI. 1955. Iron and composition, 72 in. high. Coll. Mr. A. L. Arenberg, Chicago. [Plate 143]
The Inner Eye. 1952. Iron and glass, 90½ in. high. Museum of Modern Art, New York. [Plate 144]

Sir William COLDSTREAM

Born 1908 in Belford, Northumberland. Studied at the Slade School. With Victor Pasmore and Claude Rogers founded the School of Drawing and Painting at 316 Euston Road, in 1937. Official Artist in Middle East and Italy in World War II. Slade Professor of Fine Art, London University. Trustee of the National Gallery and of the Tate Gallery. A retrospective exhibition held at The South London Gallery in 1962.

Mrs. S. G H. Burger. 1936–7. Oil, 31×22 in. Tate Gallery, London. [Plate 67]
The Studio. 1932–3. Oil, 54×36 in. In the artist's possession. [Plate 68]

Cecil COLLINS

Born 1908 in Plymouth. Studied at the Plymouth School of Art and at the Royal College of Art. First one-man exhibition in London in 1935; represented in the International Surrealist Exhibition held in London in 1936. First large-scale exhibition in London in 1944 when the gallery was damaged in an air-raid and two of his pictures were destroyed. A retrospective exhibition held at the Whitechapel Art Gallery in 1959.

Lit.: *Cecil Collins: Paintings and Drawings (1935–1945)*, with an Introduction by Alex Comfort, 1946.

Christ before the Judge. 1954. Oil, 36×48 in. Coll. The Hon. Robert Baring, London. [Plate 104]
The Sleeping Fool. 1943. Oil, 11¾×15¾ in. Tate Gallery, London [Plate 105]

Robert COLQUHOUN

Born 1914 in Kilmarnock, Ayrshire. Studied at the Glasgow School of Art, where he won a travelling scholarship which enabled him to visit France and Italy. After serving in World War II, he settled in London. First one-man exhibition in London in 1943. Designed for the theatre. Represented in the British Pavilion at the Venice Biennale in 1954. A retrospective exhibition – 1942 to 1958 – held at the Whitechapel Art Gallery in 1958.

The Fortune Teller. 1946. Oil, 50×32 in. Coll. Sir Colin Anderson, London. [Plate 148]

John CRAXTON

Born 1922 in London. Studied at Goldsmiths' College and at the Westminster School of Art. First one-man exhibition in London in 1944. Since 1946 has made frequent and prolonged visits to Greece.

Hotel by the Sea. 1946. Oil, 19½×24 in. Tate Gallery, London. [Plate 110]

Alan DAVIE

Born 1920 in Grangemouth, Scotland. Studied at the Edinburgh College of Art. Served in World War II. First one-man exhibition in Edinburgh in 1946, and in London in 1950. Abandoned painting the following year to become a professional jazz musician, but in 1948 took up a Travelling Scholarship won at Edinburgh and visited Italy (where he held one-man exhibitions in Florence and Venice), France, Switzerland and Spain. Settled in England and visited New York for his first one-man exhibition there in 1956 where he met Jackson Pollock, de Kooning and other leading American painters. Gregory Fellow at Leeds University. Retrospective exhibitions held at Wakefield, Nottingham, Liverpool and Whitechapel art galleries in 1958.

Male and Female. 1955. Oil, 78×60 in. Albright Art Gallery, Buffalo, N.Y. [Plate 154]

Roy DE MAISTRE

Born 1894 in Bowral, New South Wales, Australia. Studied at the Royal Art Society of New South Wales, and at the Sydney Art School. First one-man exhibition in Sydney in 1927 and in London in 1929; retrospective exhibitions held at Temple Newsam, Leeds, in 1943 and at the Whitechapel Art Gallery in 1960. Worked in Australia and in France. Settled in London 1938.

Noli Me Tangere. About 1951. Oil, 72×48 in. Coll. The Hon. Richard and Mrs. Rhys, London. [Plate 108]
Veiled Madonna. 1946. Oil, 48×38 in. In the artist's possession. [Plate 109]

Frank DOBSON

Born 1888 in London. Studied at the City and Guilds School, Kennington. Served in World War I. First one-man exhibition as a draughtsman in 1914 and as a sculptor in 1921. Professor of Sculpture at the Royal College of Art.

Sir Osbert Sitwell, Bt. 1923. Brass, 12½ in. high. Tate Gallery, London [Plate 93]

Sir Jacob EPSTEIN

Born 1880 in New York. After studying in Paris he settled in England in 1905. First one-man exhibition in London in 1913. Carved or modelled a long series of public monuments, the earliest being eighteen figures on the new building of the British Medical Association in the Strand, in 1908, and the Tomb of Oscar Wilde in the Cemetery of Père Lachaise, Paris, in 1911–13; also modelled many portrait busts – including a number of illustrious contemporaries – as well as numerous figures. Retrospective exhibitions held at the Tate Gallery in 1952 and 1961. Died 1959.

Lit.: *The Sculptor Speaks*, by Jacob Epstein, 1931. – *Let there be Sculpture*, by Jacob Epstein, 1940.

Isobel. 1931. Bronze, 27 in. high. Ferens Art Gallery, Kingston-upon-Hull. [Plate 38]
The Rock Drill. 1913. Bronze, 27¾ in. high. Tate Gallery, London. [Plate 39]
Madonna and Child. 1951. Lead, 13 ft. high. Convent of the Holy Child Jesus, Cavendish Square, London. [Plate 40]
Admiral of the Fleet Lord Fisher of Kilverstone, G.C.B., O.M., G.C.V.O. 1915. Bronze, 18½ in. high. Imperial War Museum, London. [Plate 41]

Lucian FREUD

Born 1922 in Berlin, grandson of Sigmund Freud. Settled in London in 1932. Studied at the Central School of Art and at Goldsmiths' College. First one-man exhibition in London in 1944. Represented in the British Pavilion at the Venice Biennale in 1954. Taught at the Slade School.

Francis Bacon. 1952. Oil, 7×5 in. Tate Gallery, London. [Plate 94]
Girl with a Rose. 1947-8. Oil, 41½×29 in. Coll. British Council, London. [Plate 95]

Elisabeth FRINK

Born 1930 in Thurlow, Suffolk. Studied at the Chelsea School of Art. First one-man exhibition in London in 1955. Taught at the Chelsea and St. Martin's Schools of Art.

Blind Man and Dog. 1958. Bronze, 72 in. and 30 in. high. Bethnal Green Borough Council. [Plate 127]

Anthony FRY

Born 1927 in Theydon Bois, Essex. Studied at Edinburgh College of Art and Camberwell School of Art. First one-man exhibition in London in 1955. Taught at the Bath Academy of Art and Camberwell School of Art. Awarded Rome Prize 1950–52: made frequent visits to Italy.

Dancing Figures, No. 3. 1958. Oil, 84×72 in. Coll. J. D. Sainsbury, Esq., London. [Plate 125]

Henri GAUDIER-BRZESKA

Born Henri Gaudier 1891 in St. Jean de Braye, near Orleans. In 1910 he decided to become a sculptor and the following year settled in England with Sophie Brzeska, with whom he lived and whose surname he added to his own. Member of the Vorticist Group, and contributed to *Blast II* "Vortex Gaudier-Brzeska", which he wrote in the trenches while serving as a sergeant in the French Army on the Western Front. Killed in action in 1915. No one-man exhibition during his life, but retrospective exhibitions held in London in 1918 and at the Arts Council Gallery, and in Orleans in 1956.

Lit.: *Gaudier-Brzeska*, by Ezra Pound, 1916. – *A Life o, Gaudier-Brzeska*, by H. S. Ede, 1930. – *Savage Messiah*, by H. S. Ede, 1931. – *Henri Gaudier-Brzeska*, by Horace Brodzky, 1933.

Sophie Brzeska. 1913. Pastel, 22×15⅛ in. Tate Gallery, London. [Plate 33]
The Dancer. 1913. Bronze, 28⅞ in. high. Coll. Mrs. Violet Schiff, London. [Plate 34]

Mark GERTLER

Born 1891 in Spitalfields, London, of a family of emigrants from Przemysl, Galicia, where they returned shortly after his birth, finally settling in London in 1898. Studied at the Slade School. First one-man exhibition in London in 1921. Taught at Westminster Art School. Died by his own hand in 1939. Retrospective exhibitions held at the Ben Uri Gallery in 1944 and at the Whitechapel Art Gallery in 1949.

Roundabout. 1916. Oil, 75½×56½ in. Ben Uri Gallery, London. [Plate 85]
Rabbi and Rabbitzen. 1914. Oil, 19×15 in. Coll. Jeremy Hutchinson, Esq., London. [Plate 86]

Eric GILL

Born 1882 in Brighton. Apprenticed to an architect; studied at the Chichester School of Art, at the Central School of Arts and Crafts under W. R. Lethaby and Edward Johnston, and at the Westminster School of Art. Began inscription writing in 1903 and figure carving in 1910. Received into the Catholic Church in 1913, becoming a Tertiary in the Third Order of St. Dominic five years later. Carved The Stations of the Cross for Westminster Cathedral and for St. Cuthbert's Catholic Church, Bradford. Typographer and writer. Died 1940.

Lit.: *Eric Gill* (Contemporary British Artists), by J. K. M. R. (Sir John Rothenstein), 1927. – *Eric Gill*, by Joseph Thorp, 1929. – *Autobiography*, 1940. – *Letters*, ed. by Walter Shewring, 1947.

Mankind. 1927–28. Hoptonwood stone, 95 in. high. Tate Gallery, London. [Plate 35]

William George GILLIES

Born 1898 in Haddington, East Lothian, Scotland. After serving in World War I he studied at the Edinburgh College of Art, where he won a scholarship that enabled him to study in Italy and France. First one-man exhibition in Edinburgh in 1948. A retrospective exhibition of his work held jointly with that of John Maxwell at the New Burlington Galleries, London, in 1954. Head of Edinburgh College of Art.

Esperston. 1950. Oil, 14×26 in. Tate Gallery, London. [Plate 55]

Harold GILMAN

Born 1876 in Road, Somerset. Studied at Hastings Art School and at the Slade School. A founder of the Camden Town Group. Exhibited in London with Gore in 1913 and with Ginner in 1914. A retrospective exhibition held at the Arts Council Gallery in 1954. Died 1919.

Lit.: *Harold Gilman: an Appreciation*, by Wyndham Lewis and Louis F. Fergusson, 1919.

Mrs. Mounter at the Breakfast Table. 1916. Oil, 23½×15½ in. Tate Gallery, London [Plate 16]
Oak Tree. About 1916. Pen drawing, 16⅝×10½ in. Coll. John Piper, Esq., Henley-on-Thames. [Plate 17]

Charles GINNER

Born 1878 in Cannes, of English parents. Studied in Paris at the Académie Vitti and at the Ecole des Beaux-Arts. First one-man exhibition in Buenos Aires in 1909; settled in London the following year. Exhibited in London with Gilman in 1914 and reprinted, as foreword to the catalogue, his essay on *Neo-Realism*. Official Artist in both World Wars. Died 1952. A retrospective exhibition held at the Tate Gallery in 1954.

The Aqueduct, Bath. 1928. Oil, 30×24 in. Coll. British Council. [Plate 20]
The Café Royal. 1911. Oil, 25×19 in. Tate Gallery, London. [Plate 22]

Spencer F. GORE

Born 1878 in Epsom, Surrey. Studied at the Slade School. First president of The Camden Gown Group, 1911. Taught at the Westminster Art School. Exhibited in London with Gilman in 1913. Died 1914. Retrospective exhibitions held in London in 1916, 1920 and 1928, and at the Arts Council Gallery in 1955.

North London Girl. 1911. Oil, 24×20 in. Tate Gallery, London. [Plate 14]

Lawrence GOWING

Born 1918 in London. Studied at the School of Drawing and Painting, Euston Road. First one-man exhibition in London in 1948. Professor of Fine Art at Durham University and Principal of the King Edward School of Art, Newcastle; Principal, Chelsea School of Art, and Trustee of the Tate Gallery. Art historian and critic.

Lady Asleep. 1945. Oil, 30×25 in. Coll. The Hon. Mrs. Henry Yorke, London. [Plate 65]

Duncan GRANT

Born 1885 in Rothiemurchus, Inverness-shire, Scotland. Studied at the Westminster School of Art, under J.-E. Blanche in Paris, in Italy, and briefly at the Slade School. Through his cousin, Lytton Strachey, entered Bloomsbury circle of Roger Fry, Clive and Vanessa Bell, Virginia Woolf. Worked with Roger Fry in the Omega Workshops. First one-man exhibition in London in 1920. Represented in the British Pavilion at the Venice Biennale in 1926 and 1932. A retrospective exhibition held at the Tate Gallery in 1959.

Lit.: *Duncan Grant*, with an Introduction by Roger Fry, 1923. – *Duncan Grant* (Penguin Modern Painters), by Raymond Mortimer, 1944.

Nude Study. 1935. Pastel, 27⅞×18½ in. Coll. Sir Kenneth Clark, Saltwood Castle, Kent. [Plate 44]
Vanessa Bell. 1942. Oil, 40×24 in. Tate Gallery, London. [Plate 63]

Derrick GREAVES

Born 1927 in Sheffield. Began to attend evening art classes while apprenticed to a sign writer; studied at the Royal College of Art, where he won a travelling scholarship which enabled him to visit Italy. First one-man exhibition in London in 1953. Taught at the St. Martin's School of Art.

Sheffield. 1953. Oil, 80×34 in. Junior Common Room, Balliol College, Oxford. [Plate 77]

Anthony GROSS

Born 1905 in London. Studied at the Slade School and at the Académie Julian, Paris. First one-man exhibition in London in 1934. Official Artist in World War II in the Middle East, India and Europe. Has illustrated books and made animated cartoons.

Gateway into Germany: the Maas in Flood near the Berg Bridge. 1944. Watercolour, 16¼×23¼ in. Tate Gallery, London [Plate 52]

Allan GWYNNE-JONES

Born 1892 in Richmond, Surrey. Studied at the Slade School. Served in World War I. First one-man exhibition in London in 1923. Taught at the Royal College of Art and the Slade School. Trustee of the Tate Gallery. Occasional writer.

Miss Diana Hunt. 1944. Oil, 14×12 in. National Gallery of New South Wales, Sydney. [Plate 66]

Stanley William HAYTER

Born 1901 in Hackney, London, son of a painter. Began to paint in spare time in 1915 while working for honours degree in chemistry at King's College, London. With Anglo-Iranian Oil Company in Abadan 1922–25; visited Iraq and Arabia. Returned to England and became professional painter in 1925 and settled in Paris the following year. Founded Atelier 17 for research in print-making and held first one-man exhibition in Paris in 1927. Associated with Calder, Arp and Tanguy; with Picasso 1934–39 to whom he gave technical assistance in print-making. In U.S.A. 1940–50, setting up Atelier 17 independently in New York in 1944. Published many prints. A retrospective exhibition held at the Whitechapel Art Gallery in 1957; represented in the British Pavilion at the Venice Biennale in 1958. Lives in Paris.

Labyrinth. 1953. Oil, 76⅝×44⅞ in. Coll. M. Nesto Jacometti, Zurich. [Plate 155]

Barbara HEPWORTH

Born 1903 in Wakefield, Yorkshire. Studied at the Leeds School of Art and at the Royal College of Art. Won a scholarship which enabled her to continue her studies in Italy. First one-man exhibition in London in 1928, in New York in 1949; retrospective exhibitions held at Temple Newsam, Leeds, in 1943, and at the Whitechapel Art Gallery in 1954. Represented in the British Pavilion at the Venice Biennale in 1950. Awarded a second prize in the International Sculpture Competition *The Unknown Political Prisoner* at the Tate Gallery in 1953, and the Grand Prize at the São Paulo Bienal in 1959. Married to Ben Nicholson.

Lit.: *Barbara Hepworth* (Ariel Series). Introduction by William Gibson, 1946. – *Barbara Hepworth – Carvings and Drawings*. Introduction by Sir Herbert Read, 1952.

Two Figures. 1947–48. Wood with white paint, 48 in. high. Coll. Mr. & Mrs. John Rood, Minneapolis. [Plate 118]

Josef HERMAN

Born 1911 in Warsaw. Studied at the Warsaw School of Art. Came to Britain in 1940. Lived in South Wales 1944 to 1953, taking his subjects from a mining village. Subsequently settled in London, where he had held his first one-man exhibition in 1947. Retrospective exhibition held at the Whitechapel Art Gallery in 1956.

Lit.: *Josef Herman: Drawings*. Introduction by Basil Taylor, 1956.

Two Miners. 1945. Pastel, 21×32½ in. Coll. Mr. Edgar Jones, Washington. [Plate 113]

Tristram HILLIER

Born 1905 in Peking. Studied at the Slade School and in Paris. First one-man exhibition in London in 1931. Lived in France for several years before World War II and briefly after it. Has worked in Spain and Portugal.

Lit.: *Leda and the Goose* (an autobiography). 1954.

Viseu. 1947. Oil, 24×32 in. Coll. Major E. O. Kay, Hove. [Plate 78]

Ivon HITCHENS

Born 1893 in London, son of Alfred Hitchens, painter. Studied at the St. John's Wood School of Art and at the Royal Academy Schools. First one-man exhibition in London in 1925. Retrospective exhibitions held at Temple Newsam, Leeds, in 1945, Graves Art Gallery, Sheffield, in 1948, and in the British Pavilion at the Venice Biennale in 1956.

Lit.: *Ivon Hitchens* (Penguin Modern Painters), by Patrick Heron, 1955.

Millpool, Coming Storm. 1951. Oil, 17×43 in. Coll. Howard Bliss, Esq., London. [Plate 123]
Waterfall, Terwick Mill. 1945. Oil, 16×29¼ in. Coll. Sir Selwyn Selwyn-Clarke, London. [Plate 124]

Frances HODGKINS

Born 1869 in Dunedin, New Zealand. Studied with her father, an amateur artist, and at the Dunedin School of Art. From 1901 she lived chiefly in Europe, making Paris her headquarters, but travelling widely and frequently. Taught at the Atelier Colarossi, Paris, and held classes on her own. First one-man exhibitions in London in 1907, in Melbourne in 1912 and in Wellington in 1913. Died 1947. Memorial exhibitions held in the City Art Gallery, Manchester, in 1947, in the Isle of Purbeck, in 1948, and in London in 1949. Retrospective exhibitions held in London in 1946 and, with Ethel Walker and Gwen John, at the Tate Gallery in 1952.

Lit.: *Frances Hodgkins* (Penguin Modern Painters), by Myfanwy Evans, 1948. – *Frances Hodgkins: Four Vital Years*, by Arthur R. Howell, 1951. – *Works of Frances Hodgkins in New Zealand*, by E. H. McCormick, 1954.

Broken Tractor. About 1942. Gouache, 14½×21½ in. Tate Gallery, London. [Plate 11]

Albertus Antonius HOUTHUESEN

Born 1903 in Amsterdam; brought to England as a child. Studied at the St. Martin's School of Art and at the Royal College of Art. Married Catherine Dean, a painter. First one-man exhibition in London in 1961.

Trees in Ruskin Park. 1960. Chalk drawing. 18¼×27¼ in. Coll. Sir John Rothenstein, Newington. [Plate 57]
The Supper at Emmaus. 1927–28. Oil, 30¾×42½ in. Coll. Sir John Rothenstein, Newington. [Plate 58]

James Dickson INNES

Born 1887 in Llanelly, Carmarthenshire, Wales. Studied at Carmarthen Art School and at the Slade School. Worked largely in the Pyrenees, Spain and North Wales. First exhibition (with Eric Gill) in London in 1911. Died 1914. Retrospective exhibitions held at the Tate Gallery in 1921–22 and at the Graves Art Gallery, Sheffield, in 1961.

Lit.: *James Dickson Innes*, with an Introduction to the reproductions by John Fothergill, collected and edited by Lillian Browse, 1948.

The Waterfall. 1910. Watercolour, 10¼×14½ in. Tate Gallery, London. [Plate 48]

Robin IRONSIDE

Born 1912 in London. Studied at the Courtauld Institute but self-taught as a painter. First exhibition (with Christopher Ironside) in London in 1944; first one-man

exhibition in New York in 1949. Assistant Keeper, Tate Gallery, and Assistant Secretary, Contemporary Art Society. Art historian.

Visitor to a Museum Posing on a Vacant Plinth. 1955. Watercolour, 20×30 in. Coll. The Hon. Mrs. Rayner, London. [Plate 111]

Augustus JOHN

Born 1878 in Tenby, Wales. Studied at the Slade School. First one-man exhibition in London in 1903. Professor of Painting at Liverpool University and Trustee of the Tate Gallery. A retrospective exhibition of his drawings held at the National Gallery in 1940: others of wider scope held at the National Eisteddfod of Wales, in 1948, and at the Royal Academy in the Diploma Gallery, Burlington House, in 1954. Died 1961.

Lit.: *Augustus John* (Contemporary British Artists) by A. B. (Anthony Bertram), 1923. – *Augustus John Drawings*, edited by Lillian Browse, 1941. – *Augustus John* (Phaidon British Artists), by Sir John Rothenstein, 1944. – *Chiaroscuro: fragments of autobiography*, by Augustus John, 1952.

Lady Ottoline Morrell. 1926. Oil, 26×19 in. Coll. Mrs. Julian Vinogradoff, London. [Plate 27]
Dorelia in Eastern Dress. About 1906. Watercolour, 17½× 10 in. Coll. Mrs. Dudley Tooth, London. [Plate 28]
His Honour H. C. Dowdall, K.C., as Lord Mayor of Liverpool. 1908–9. Oil, 80×53 in. National Gallery of Victoria, Melbourne. [Plate 29]
Two Children. About 1900–1908. Pencil drawing, 9×6½ in. Coll. T. H. Priestley, Esq., London. [Plate 30]
Daphne. 1937. Oil, 16×13¾ in. Coll. Lady Mary Campbell, Great Bedwin. [Plate 31]
Portrait Head of a Woman. About 1904. Charcoal, 12× 10 in. Coll. Colonel Robert D. Q. Henriques, Winson. [Plate 32]

Gwen JOHN

Born 1876 in Haverfordwest, Pembrokeshire, Wales; sister of Augustus John. Studied at the Slade School and at Whistler's School in Paris. A friend of Rodin, and Rilke. Received into the Catholic Church in 1913. Lived mostly in France. Showed her work rarely; held her only one-man exhibition, in London, in 1926. Died 1939. Retrospective exhibitions held in London in 1946, and with Ethel Walker and Frances Hodgkins at the Tate Gallery in 1952.

Girl in Profile. About 1920. Oil, 17¾×12½ in. National Museum of Wales, Cardiff. [Plate 15]

David JONES

Born 1895 in Brockley, Kent, of Welsh descent on his father's side. Studied at Camberwell School of Art and, after service in World War I, at the Westminster School of Art. Received into the Catholic Church in 1921, joining Eric Gill's Guild of St. Joseph and St. Dominic at Ditchling,

Sussex. First one-man exhibition in London in 1929. Represented in the British Pavilion at the Venice Biennale in 1934. A retrospective exhibition held at Aberystwyth, Cardiff, and Swansea, at the Royal Scottish Academy and at the Tate Gallery in 1954–55. Imaginative writer of distinction.

Lit.: *David Jones* (Penguin Modern Painters), by Robin Ironside, 1949. – *In Parenthesis*, by David Jones, 1937.

Aphrodite in Aulis. 1941. Pen and watercolour, 24⅜×19¼ in. Private Collection. [Plate 96]

Eric KENNINGTON

Born 1888 in Chelsea, son of the painter T. B. Kennington. Studied at the Lambeth and the Kennington Schools of Art. First one-man exhibition in London in 1916. Served in World War I and as Official Artist in both I and II. Visited Arabia in 1920 with T. E. Lawrence, of whom he made recumbent effigies for Warham Church, Dorset, and for the Tate Gallery, and of whose *Seven Pillars of Wisdom* he was art editor. Died 1961.

Lit.: *Drawing the R.A.F.*, by Eric Kennington, 1942.

Recumbent Figure of T. E. Lawrence. 1939–1954. Ciment fondu, 82½ in. long. Tate Gallery, London. [Plate 42]
Muttar il Hamoud Min Beni Hassan. 1920. Pastel, 30¼×22 in. Tate Gallery, London. [Plate 43]

Henry LAMB

Born 1885 in Adelaide, Australia. Abandoned medicine for painting, and studied at La Palette, Paris. Served in World War I and as Official Artist in World War II. First one-man exhibition in London in 1922. Trustee of the Tate Gallery and of the National Portrait Gallery. Died 1961.

Lit.: *Henry Lamb* (Contemporary British Artists), by G. L. K. (G. L. Kennedy), 1924.

Lytton Strachey. 1914. Oil, 96×70¼ in. Tate Gallery, London. [Plate 64]

Peter LANYON

Born 1918 in St. Ives, Cornwall. Studied at the Penzance School of Art, the School of Drawing and Painting, Euston Road, and with Ben Nicholson; also encouraged by Naum Gabo. First one-man exhibition in London in 1949, and in New York in 1959. Represented at São Paulo Bienal in 1961. Served in World War II in Middle East and Italy.

Sand Bar. 1956. Oil, 6×4 ft. Coll. Mr. Thomas Adler, Chicago. [Plate 153]

Edward LE BAS

Born 1904 in London, of Channel Island descent. After

taking a degree in architecture at Cambridge studied painting at the Royal College of Art. First one-man exhibition in London in 1936. Travelled widely.

Interior. 1951. Oil, 36¼×65¼ in. Tate Gallery, London. [Plate 59]

Wyndham LEWIS

Born 1882 (1884 and 1886 have until recently been the generally accepted dates) on his father's yacht in the Bay of Fundy, Nova Scotia. Studied at the Slade School, at the Heimann Academy, Munich, and in Paris, Holland and Spain. Founded the Vorticist Group, 1914–15, and edited its journal "Blast". Served in World War I, also as Official Artist to the Canadian Army. First one-man exhibition in London in 1919, and a retrospective exhibition "Wyndham Lewis and Vorticism" held at the Tate Gallery in 1956. Philosopher and critic, writer of novels and trilogy for broadcasting, "The Human Age". Lost his sight 1951. Died 1957.

Lit.: *Blasting and Bombardiering* (autobiography), by Wyndham Lewis, 1937. – *Wyndham Lewis the Artist: Essays on Art*, by Wyndham Lewis, 1939. – *Rude Assignment* (autobiography) by Wyndham Lewis, 1950. – *The Art of Wyndham Lewis*, edited by Charles Handley-Read, 1951. – *Wyndham Lewis: A portrait of the Artist as the Enemy*, by Geoffrey Wagner, 1957.

Portrait of a Girl Standing. 1920. Black chalk, 16½×10 in. City Art Gallery, Rutherston Collection, Manchester. [Plate 69]
Edith Sitwell. 1923–35. Oil, 34×44 in. Tate Gallery, London [Plate 70]
Revolution. About 1917. Oil, 78×60 in. Marlborough Gallery, London. [Plate 71]

L. S. LOWRY

Born 1887 in Old Trafford, Manchester. Studied at the Art Schools of Manchester and Salford. First one-man exhibition in London in 1939 and in Manchester in 1948. Has always lived in the neighbourhood of Manchester, first at Pendlebury and later at Mottram in Longdendale. A retrospective exhibition held in the Salford Art Gallery in 1951.

Lit.: *The Discovery of L. S. Lowry*, by Maurice Collis, 1951. *L. S. Lowry*, by Mervyn Levy, 1961.

River Scene. 1942. Oil, 18½×25¾ in. Glasgow Art Gallery and Museum. [Plate 50]

Robert MACBRYDE

Born 1913 in Maybole, Ayrshire, but has lived in England since 1939. Studied at the Glasgow School of Art and abroad after spending five years in a factory and an engineering works. First exhibition in London with Robert

Colquhoun – with whom he has been closely associated – in 1944. With Colquhoun he has also designed for the theatre.

Woman with Paper Flower. 1944. Oil, 21×27¾ in. Tate Gallery, London. [Plate 149]

Ambrose McEVOY

Born 1878 in Crudwell, Wiltshire. Studied at the Slade School. First one-man exhibition New York in 1920 and in London in 1923. Served in World War I. Died 1927.

Lit.: *Ambrose McEvoy* (Contemporary British Artists), by R. M. Y. G. (R. M. Y. Gleadowe), 1924.

The Hon. Daphne Baring. 1916. Oil, 42½×32½ in. Coll. The Hon. Mrs. Arthur Pollen, London. [Plate 26]

F. E. McWILLIAM

Born 1909 at Banbridge, Northern Ireland. Studied at the Slade School and in Paris. First one-man exhibition in London in 1939.

Princess Macha. 1957. Bronze, 96 in. high. Altnagelvin Hospital, Londonderry. [Plate 142]

Charles MAHONEY

Born 1903 in London. Studied at the Royal College of Art. Carried out large wall paintings at Morley College (destroyed in World War II) and in the Lady Chapel, Campion Hall, Oxford. Taught at the Royal College of Art and at the Byam Shaw School of Art.

The Nativity. About 1950. Oil, 103×72 in. Campion Hall, Oxford. [Plate 60]

John MAXWELL

Born 1905 in Dalbeattie, Kirkudbrightshire. Studied at the Edinburgh College of Art and in Paris, at the Académie Moderne, under Léger and Ozenfant. Taught at the Edinburgh College of Art for ten years, retiring to his native place in 1946. A retrospective exhibition of his work together with that of Gillies held at the New Burlington Galleries in 1954.

Landscape with Dead Trees. 1947. Watercolour, 18¾×21 in. Coll. Dr. Harold Fletcher, Edinburgh. [Plate 106]
Woman with Flowers. 1941. Oil, 31×21¼ in. Coll. Gordon Small, Esq., Edinburgh. [Plate 107]

Bernard MEADOWS

Born 1915 in Norwich. Studied at the Royal College of Art. Served in World War II. Worked as an assistant to Henry Moore. First one-man exhibition in London in 1957. Represented in the British Pavilion at the Venice Biennale in 1952. Taught at the Chelsea School of Art and at the Bath Academy of Art.

The Crab. 1954. Bronze, 13 in. high. Jesus College, Cambridge. [Plate 145]

Edward MIDDLEDITCH

Born 1923 in Chelmsford, Essex. Studied at the Regent Street Polytechnic, and at the Royal College of Art. First one-man exhibition in London in 1954. Represented in the British Pavilion at the Venice Biennale in 1956. Taught painting at the Chelsea Polytechnic and at the St. Martin's School of Art.

Pigeons in Trafalgar Square. 1954. Oil, 72×48 in. Leicestershire County Council. [Plate 112]

John MINTON

Born 1917 near Cambridge. Studied at the St. John's Wood School of Art, and in Paris. Served (after a period as a conscientious objector) in World War II. First one-man exhibition in London in 1945. Taught in the Painting School at the Royal College of Art for the last eight years of his life. Designed for the theatre. Travelled widely around the Mediterranean and in the West Indies. Died by his own hand in 1957.

Street and Railway Bridge. 1946. Oil, 18×24 in. Tate Gallery, London. [Plate 79]

Henry MOORE

Born 1898 in Castleford, Yorkshire, the seventh child of a coal miner. After serving in World War I he abandoned school teaching and studied at the Leeds School of Art and at the Royal College of Art, winning a travelling scholarship which enabled him to visit Italy and France. Official Artist in World War II. First one-man exhibition in London in 1928. Many retrospective exhibitions have been held, among others at Temple Newsam, Leeds, in 1941, in the British Pavilion at the Venice Biennale (where he won the International Sculpture Prize) in 1948, at the Musée d'Art Moderne, Paris, in 1949, at the Tate Gallery in 1951, at the São Paulo Bienal (where he won the International Prize for Sculpture) in 1953–54. Taught at the Royal College of Art and at the Chelsea School of Art. Trustee of the Tate Gallery and of the National Gallery.

Lit.: *Henry Moore* (Penguin Modern Painters), by Geoffrey Grigson, 1943. – *Henry Moore: sculpture and drawings,* with an Introduction by Sir Herbert Read, 1944, 1946, 1949 (revised and enlarged). – *Henry Moore, Volume II: sculpture and drawings since 1948,* with an Introduction by Sir Herbert Read, 1955. – *Henry Moore,* by James Johnson Sweeney, New York, 1946. – *Henry Moore,* by Giulio Carlo Argan, Turin, 1948.

Pink and Green Sleepers. 1941. Wash and crayon, 22×15 in. Tate Gallery, London. [Plate 114]
Two-piece Reclining Figure No. 2. 1960. Bronze, 102 in. high. Tate Gallery, London. [Plate 115]

King and Queen. 1952–3. Bronze, 64½ in. high. Coll. W. J. Keswick, Esq., Shawhead. [Plate 116]
Helmet Head No. 2. 1950. Bronze, 15½ in. high. National Gallery of New South Wales, Sydney. [Plate 117]

Rodrigo MOYNIHAN

Born 1910 in Teneriffe, Canary Islands; brought to England at the age of eight. Studied in Rome and at the Slade School. First one-man exhibition in London in 1940. Served in the forces and as Official Artist in World War II. Professor of Painting at the Royal College of Art.

The Teaching Staff of the Royal College of Art. 1951. Oil, 84×132 in. Tate Gallery, London. [Plate 61]

John NASH

Born 1893 in London. Attended no art school but was encouraged by his brother Paul Nash, with whom he held his first exhibition in London in 1913. First one-man exhibition in London in 1921. Served in the forces and as Official Artist in both World Wars. Taught at the Ruskin School of Drawing, Oxford, and at the Royal College of Art. Illustrated some twenty-six books, mostly with coloured lithographs or wood engravings.

Winter Afternoon. 1945. Watercolour, 14⅞×21⅛ in. City Art Gallery, Birmingham. [Plate 51]

Paul NASH

Born 1889 in London. Studied at Bolt Court, Fleet Street, and at the Slade School. First one-man exhibition in London in 1912. Served in the forces and as Official Artist in both World Wars. Founded Unit One in 1933. Illustrated seventeen books, and was an occasional writer. Died 1946. A retrospective exhibition held at the Tate Gallery in 1948.

Lit.: *Paul Nash* (Contemporary British Artists), by A. B. (Anthony Bertram), 1923. – *Paul Nash* (Penguin Modern Painters), by Sir Herbert Read, 1944. – *Paul Nash*, Paintings, Drawings and Illustrations, with contributions by Sir Herbert Read, Sir John Rothenstein, E. H. Ramsden, Philip James and Richard Seddon, edited by Margot Eates, 1948. – *Outline, an autobiography and other writings*, by Paul Nash, with a preface by Sir Herbert Read, 1949. – *Paul Nash, The Portrait of an Artist*, by Anthony Bertram, 1955.

Northern Adventure. 1929. Oil, 36×28 in. Aberdeen Art Gallery. [Plate 72]
Landscape of the Vernal Equinox. 1943. Oil, 28×36 in. Coll. H.M. Queen Elizabeth The Queen Mother. [Plate 73]
Monster Field. 1939. Oil, 30×40 in. Durban Museum and Art Gallery, South Africa. [Plate 74]

C. R. W. NEVINSON

Born 1889 in London. Studied at the St. John's Wood and the Slade Schools and in Paris at the Académie Julian

and the Cercle Russe. Published manifesto "Vital English Art" with Marinetti in 1914. Official Artist in World War I. First one-man exhibition in London in 1916. Died 1946.

Lit.: *C. R. W. Nevinson* (Contemporary British Artists), by O. S. (Sir Osbert Sitwell, Bt.), 1925. – *Paint and Prejudice* (autobiography), 1937.

Column on the March. 1915. Oil, 29½×24 in. Coll. L. J. Cadbury, Esq., Birmingham. [Plate 80]
La Patrie. 1916. Oil, 23½×35½ in. Coll. L. J. Cadbury, Esq., Birmingham. [Plate 81]

Ben NICHOLSON

Born 1894 in Denham, Buckinghamshire, eldest son of Sir William Nicholson. Studied briefly at the Slade School. Married Winifred Roberts, painter, and subsequently Barbara Hepworth, sculptor. First one-man exhibition in London in 1922. Retrospective exhibitions held at Temple Newsam, Leeds, in 1944, in the British Pavilion at the Venice Biennale (where he was awarded the "Ulissi" prize) in 1954, and subsequently at the Tate Gallery in 1955. Won Guggenheim Award for Painting, 1956.

Lit.: *Ben Nicholson, paintings, reliefs, drawings*, with an introduction by Sir Herbert Read, 1948. – *Ben Nicholson, Work since 1949* (vol. II). Introduction by Sir Herbert Read, 1956. – *Ben Nicholson*, by J. P. Hodin, 1957.

St. Ives, 1940. Oil, 12¾×15⅝ in. Coll. C. S. Reddihough, Esq., Ilkley. [Plate 134]
Porthmeor, St. Ives, 1928. Oil, 36×48 in. Coll. Miss Helen Sutherland, Penrith. [Plate 135]
Painted Relief 1939 (version 1). Oil, 33×45 in. Museum of Modern Art, New York. [Plate 136]

Sir William NICHOLSON

Born 1872 in Newark-on-Trent. Studied at Herkomer's School, Bushey, and at the Académie Julian, Paris. Collaborated with James Pryde, whose sister Mabel he had married, in designing posters under the name "J. & W. Beggarstaff". First one-man exhibition in London in 1911. Retrospective exhibitions held in Nottingham in 1933, and (with J. B. Yeats) at the National Gallery in 1942. Trustee of the Tate Gallery. Died 1949.

Lit.: *William Nicholson* (Contemporary British Artists), by S. K. N. (Kennedy North), 1923. – *William Nicholson*, by Marguerite Steen, 1943. – *William Nicholson* (Penguin Modern Painters), by Robert Nichols, 1948. – *William Nicholson*, by Lillian Browse, 1956.

Silver. 1938. Oil, 17¼×22½ in. Tate Gallery, London. [Plate 12]

Uli NIMPTSCH

Born 1897 in Charlottenburg, Berlin. Studied at the School of Applied Art and at the Academy, Berlin. Lived in Rome and Paris, and settled in England in 1939. First one-man exhibition in London in 1942. Retrospective exhibitions held at Temple Newsam, Leeds, in 1944 and at Liverpool in 1957.

Olympia. 1953–56. Bronze, 43½ in. long. Tate Gallery, London. [Plate 37]

Sidney NOLAN

Born 1917 in Melbourne, Australia. Began to paint in 1938. First one-man exhibition in Melbourne in 1940, and in London in 1951. Commissioned by Serge Lifar to make designs for ballet *Icarus*, 1941. Served in the Australian forces in World War II. Since 1950 has spent much time travelling in Europe, especially in the Mediterranean countries, and America, making his headquarters in London. A retrospective exhibition – 1947 to 1957 – held at the Whitechapel Art Gallery in 1957.

Ram caught in a Flood. 1955. Ripolin on masonite, 36×48 in. Coll. Mrs. Cynthia Nolan, London. [Plate 121]

Sir William ORPEN

Born 1878 in Stillorgan, County Dublin. Studied at the Municipal School of Art, Dublin, and at the Slade School. First one-man exhibition in London in 1912. Official Artist in World War I and at the ensuing Peace Conference. Died 1931.

Lit.: *William Orpen* (Contemporary British Artists), by R. P. (R. Pickle), 1923. – *Sir William Orpen, Artist and Man*, by P. G. Konody and Sidney Dark, 1932.

Hommage à Manet. 1910. Oil, 62×51 in. City Art Gallery, Manchester. [Plate 23]

Eduardo PAOLOZZI

Born 1924 in Edinburgh. Studied at the Slade School and in Paris. Served in World War II. First one-man exhibition in London in 1947. Commissioned in 1953 by the City Council to design a large fountain for a new park in Hamburg. Represented in the British Pavilion at the Venice Biennale in 1952. Awarded David E. Bright Prize when his sculpture was shown in the British Pavilion at the Venice Biennale in 1960. Has made collages, lithographs, and designed wallpapers, etc. Taught at the St. Martin's School of Art, and at the Central School of Arts and Crafts.

Jason 1956. Bronze, 66½ in. high. Museum of Modern Art, New York. [Plate 146]

Victor PASMORE

Born 1908 in Chelsham, Surrey. Attended evening classes at the Central School of Arts and Crafts, while working for the London County Council. With William Coldstream, Graham Bell and Claude Rogers, founded the School of Painting and Drawing at 316 Euston Road, in 1937. First one-man exhibition in London in 1940 and retrospective exhibitions at the Institute of Contemporary Arts, London, in 1954 and at the Venice Biennale in 1960. Master of Painting, Durham University.

Evening – Hammersmith (Chiswick Reach). 1943. Oil, 34¼×47¼ in. National Gallery of Canada, Ottawa (Massey Collection). [Plate 53]
Linear Motif, Black and White. 1960–1. Oil and gravure on formica, 48¾×48¾ in. Tate Gallery, London. [Plate 139]

John PIPER

Born 1903 in Epsom, Surrey. Studied at the Richmond School of Art and the Royal College of Art. First one-man exhibition in London in 1938. Has made prints, illustrated books and designed stained glass; has also designed for opera and ballet. Trustee of the Tate Gallery.

Lit.: *John Piper* (Penguin Modern Painters), by John Betjeman, 1944. – *John Piper: Paintings, Drawings and Theatre Designs, 1932–54*, arranged and with an introduction by S. John Woods, 1955.

Hovingham Hall, Yorkshire. 1944. Watercolour, 21×28 in. Coll. Sir William Worsley, Bt., Hovingham Hall. [Plate 75]
Monument at Waldershare. 1947, Watercolour, 24×18 in. Coll. S. John Woods, Esq., London. [Plate 76]

Lucien PISSARRO

Born 1863 in Paris, eldest son of Camille Pissarro, with whom he studied. Foundation Member of the Camden Town Group 1911. Exhibited with the Impressionists in 1886. First one-man exhibition in London in 1913. First came to England in 1870; settled 1890; naturalized 1916. The last important exhibition held in his lifetime was "Three Generations of Pissarros", in which his father and daughter Orovida were represented, in 1943 at Millers, Lewes, Sussex. Designed, printed and illustrated books. Died 1944.

Ivy Cottage, Coldharbour. 1916. Oil, 20×24½ in. Tate Gallery, London [Plate 9]

Alan REYNOLDS

Born 1926 near Newmarket, Suffolk. Served in World War II. Studied briefly in Hanover and Göttingen, and at the Royal College of Art. First one-man exhibition in London in 1952. Awarded a prize at the "Giovani Pittori" exhibition, Rome, in 1954. Taught at the Central School of Arts and Crafts.

Upright Design. 1956. Gouache, 23¾×17¼ in. Coll. Sir John Rothenstein, Newington. [Plate 122]

Ceri RICHARDS

Born 1903 in Dunvant, near Swansea. Studied at Swansea School of Art and at the Royal College of Art. First one-man exhibition in London in 1942. A reprospective exhibition held at the Whitechapel Art Gallery in 1960. Designed for the theatre. Taught at the Royal College of Art. Trustee of the Tate Gallery.

Two Females. 1937. Wood collage, 63×46×3⅛ in. Tate Gallery, London. [Plate 140]
Falling Forms. 1944. Oil, 20×24 in. In the artist's possession. [Plate 141]

William ROBERTS

Born 1895 in London. Studied at the St. Martin's School of Art and at the Slade School. Worked briefly at the Omega Workshops with Roger Fry. Associated with the Vorticist movement. First one-man exhibition in London in 1923. Official Artist in both World Wars.

The Gas Chamber. 1918. Pencil and water-colour, 12½× 20 in. Imperial War Museum, London. [Plate 126]

Ivor ROBERTS-JONES

Born 1916 at Oswestry. Studied at Goldsmiths' College and the Royal Academy Schools. Served in World War II in Burma. First one-man exhibition in London in 1957. Taught at Goldsmiths' College.

Claudel. About 1956-9. Bronze, 10¼ in. high. Tate Gallery, London. [Plate 128]

Claude ROGERS

Born 1907 in London. Studied at the Slade School. First one-man exhibition in London in 1933. With Victor Pasmore, Graham Bell and William Coldstream, founded the School of Drawing and Painting at 316 Euston Road, in 1937. Served in World War II. President of the London Group 1952. Taught at the Slade School.

The Blowlamp. 1954. Oil, 24½×29½ in. Tate Gallery, London. [Plate 100]

Michael ROTHENSTEIN

Born 1908 in London, son of Sir William Rothenstein. Studied at the Central School of Arts and Crafts. First one-man exhibition in London in 1941. Taught at the Camberwell School of Art. Turned to print making in 1954.

Boat and Rocks. 1958. Mixed media, 25×24½ in. In the artist's possession. [Plate 152]

Sir William ROTHENSTEIN

Born 1872 in Bradford, Yorkshire. Studied at the Slade School and at the Académie Julian, Paris. First exhibition (with Charles Conder) in Paris in 1891, and first one-man exhibition in London in 1900. Visited India 1910. Official Artist in both World Wars; Principal of the Royal College of Art and Trustee of the Tate Gallery. Represented in the British Pavilion at the Venice Biennale in 1930. Died 1945. A retrospective exhibition held at the Tate Gallery

in 1950, and shown in an abbreviated form in Bradford and other cities.

Lit.: *William Rothenstein* (Contemporary British Artists), by H. W. (Hubert Wellington), 1923. - *Men and Memories, I,* by Sir William Rothenstein, 1931. - *Men and Memories, II,* by Sir William Rothenstein, 1932. - *Since Fifty,* by Sir William Rothenstein, 1939. - *William Rothenstein,* by Robert Speaight, 1962.

Blasted Trees, Western Front. 1918. Oil, 39¾×30 in. Coll. Sir John Rothenstein, Newington. [Plate 18]
The Church of St. Seine l'Abbaye. 1906. Oil, 29½×21½ in. City Art Gallery, Manchester. [Plate 19]

Albert RUTHERSTON

Born 1881 in Bradford, Yorkshire; brother of Sir William Rothenstein. Studied at the Slade School. First one-man exhibition in London in 1910. Served in World War I. From about 1911 turned largely to design for theatre and ballet and the decorative arts, and to book illustration. Ruskin Master of Drawing at Oxford University. Died 1953.

Lit.: *Albert Rutherston* (Contemporary British Artists), by R. M. Y. G. (R. M. Y. Gleadowe), 1925.

The Confessions of Claude. 1901. Oil, 38×29½ in. Slade School of Art, University College, London. [Plate 62]

William SCOTT

Born 1913 in Greenock, Scotland, but brought up in Northern Ireland. Studied at the Belfast College of Art and the Royal Academy Schools. First one-man exhibition in London in 1942. Served in World War II. Senior Painting Master at the Bath Academy of Art. Represented in the British Pavilion at the Venice Biennale in 1958, and the São Paulo Bienal in 1961.

Winter Still Life. 1956. Oil, 36×60 in. Tate Gallery, London. [Plate 137]
Nearing Circles. 1961. Oil, 63×68 in. Hanover Gallery, London. [Plate 138]

Walter Richard SICKERT

Born 1860 in Munich, son of O. A. Sickert, painter and illustrator. Brought to England in 1868. Studied briefly at the Slade School and under Whistler. Frequently visited Venice. Lived in Dieppe 1900 to 1905 when he settled in Fitzroy Street, where his studio became a unique meeting place for painters of the younger generation. A founder of the Camden Town Group, 1911. First one-man exhibition in London in 1895. An inveterate teacher, mostly at private classes, and an acute and entertaining occasional critic. Retrospective exhibitions held at the National Gallery in 1941 and at the Tate Gallery in 1960. Died 1942.

Lit.: *The Life and Opinions of Walter Richard Sickert,* by Robert Emmons, 1941. - *Sickert,* edited by Lillian Browse, with an essay by R. H. Wilenski, 1943. – *A Free House*, by W. R. Sickert, edited by Sir Osbert Sitwell, Bt., 1947.

The Lady in the Gondola. 1905–6. Oil, 20¾×16¼ in. Coll. Martin Halperin, Esq., London. [Plate 1]
St. Jacques, Dieppe. 1900. Oil, 21½×18 in. City Art Gallery, Birmingham. [Plate 2]
The Horses of St. Mark's. 1901. Oil, 24½×19 in. Coll. The Countess of Crawford and Balcarres, Colinsburgh. [Plate 3]
The Baby Grand. About 1914. Pencil and black chalk, 13×11 in. Executors of the late Morton Sands, London. [Plate 4]
Study for "Ennui". About 1913. Pen and chalk, 14⅝×10½ in. Ashmolean Museum, Oxford. [Plate 5]

Jack SMITH

Born 1928 in Sheffield. Studied at the Royal College of Art. First one-man exhibition in London in 1953. Visited Spain. Represented in the British Pavilion at the Venice Biennale in 1956. Taught at the Bath Academy of Art. Awarded First Prize, "John Moores Exhibition", Liverpool, in 1957.

Creation and Crucifixion. 1956. Oil, 96×120 in. Walker Art Gallery, Liverpool. [Plate 99]
Waves of Light over Glasses. 1958. Oil, 60×60 in. In the artist's possession. [Plate 102]

Sir Matthew SMITH

Born 1879 in Halifax, Yorkshire. Studied design at the Manchester School of Art and painting at the Slade School, and briefly with Matisse in Paris. First one-man exhibition in London in 1926. Represented in the British Pavilion at the Venice Biennale in 1938 and 1950. Retrospective exhibitions held at Temple Newsam, Leeds, in 1942, at the Tate Gallery in 1953 and at the Royal Academy in 1960. Died 1959.

Lit.: *Matthew Smith* (Penguin Modern Painters), by Sir Philip Hendy, 1944.

Model à la rose. 1925. Oil, 35¾×25½ in. Coll. F. W. Halliday, Esq., Shrewsbury. [Plate 45]
Fitzroy Street Nude, No. 2. 1916. Oil, 40×30 in. Coll. The British Council. [Plate 46]
Winter in Provence. About 1937. Oil, 21½×25½ in. Coll. Sir Robert Adeane, London. [Plate 47]

Sir Stanley SPENCER

Born 1891 in Cookham, Berkshire. Studied at the Slade School. Served in Macedonia in World War I. First one-man exhibition in London in 1927. Officially commissioned to paint pictures of Glasgow shipyards during World War II. Visited China in 1954. Retrospective exhibitions held at Temple Newsam, Leeds, in 1947, of his paintings at the Tate Gallery and of his drawings at the Arts Council Gallery, in 1955. Died 1959.

Lit.: *Stanley Spencer* (Contemporary British Artists) by R.H.W. (R. H. Wilenski), 1924. – *Stanley Spencer* (Phaidon British Artists), by Elizabeth Rothenstein, 1945. – *Stanley Spencer* (Penguin Modern Painters), by Eric Newton, 1947. – *Stanley Spencer*, by Maurice Collis, 1962.

Beatitudes of Love II. Knowing. 1938. Oil, 26×22 in. Coll. R. A. B. Mynors, Esq., Oxford. [Plate 87]
Resurrection, Salonika Front. 1928–9. Oil, 21×17½ ft. Oratory of All Souls, Burghclere. [Plate 88]
Zacharias and Elizabeth. 1912–13. Oil, 60×60 in. Coll. Mrs. Mary Bone, London. [Plate 89]
Joachim among the Shepherds. 1912. Pen and wash, 15×20 in. Tate Gallery, London. [Plate 90]
The Visitation. 1913. Oil, 17×17 in. Coll. James Wood, Esq., London. [Plate 91]
Self-Portrait. 1913. Oil, 24¾×20 in. Tate Gallery, London. [Plate 92]

Philip Wilson STEER

Born 1860 in Birkenhead, son of Philip Steer, painter and drawing master. Studied at Gloucester School of Art, and in Paris at the Académie Julian and the Ecole des Beaux-Arts. A foundation member and life-long exhibitor at the New English Art Club. First one-man exhibition in London in 1894. Taught at the Slade School. Died 1942. Retrospective exhibitions held at the Tate Gallery in 1929, at the National Gallery in 1943, at Temple Newsam, Leeds, in 1944, and in Birkenhead in 1951.

Lit.: *Wilson Steer* (Phaidon British Artists), by Robin Ironside, 1943. – *Philip Wilson Steer*, by D. S. McColl, 1945.

The Horseshoe Bend of the Severn. 1909. Oil, 39½ × 59 in. Art Gallery, Aberdeen. [Plate 6]
The Home Farm. 1901. Oil, 22×27 in. Executors of the late Geoffrey Blackwell, London. [Plate 7]
Mrs. Raynes. 1922. Oil, 27×22 in. Tate Gallery, London. [Plate 8]

Graham SUTHERLAND

Born 1903 in London. Studied at Goldsmiths' College. First one-man exhibition of drawings and engravings in London in 1925. Began experimenting in oils in 1930; decided to become a painter in 1935. Official Artist in World War II, he drew scenes of bomb devastation and work in mines and foundries. Among his principal retrospective exhibitions were those held in the British Pavilion at the Venice Biennale in 1952, at the Musée National d'Art Moderne, Paris, in 1952, and at the Tate Gallery in 1953. An occasional portrait painter since 1949; has designed tapestry, ceramics and for the ballet. Visiting instructor in Painting at Goldsmiths' College and Trustee of the Tate Gallery.

Lit.: *Graham Sutherland*, by Edward Sackville-West (Penguin Modern Painters), 1943; revised edition, 1955. – *Graham Sutherland*, by Robert Melville, 1950. – *The Work of Graham Sutherland*, by Douglas Cooper, 1961.

Three Standing Forms in a Garden, II. 1952. Oil, 52⅜×45⅜ in. Coll. Mrs. Graham Sutherland, West Malling. [Plate 119]
Blasted Oak. 1941. Pen and wash, 15×21 in. Coll. Sir Colin Anderson, London. [Plate 120]

Henry TONKS

Born 1862 in Solihull, Warwickshire. Abandoned medicine to become a painter. Studied at the Westminster School of Art. Joined the staff of the Slade School in 1893; Professor from 1918 until 1930. Visited Archangel, Russia, as Official Artist in World War I. A retrospective exhibition held at the Tate Gallery in 1936. Died 1937.

Lit.: *Henry Tonks*, by Joseph Hone, 1938.

Sodales – Mr. Steer and Mr. Sickert. 1930. Oil, 13¾×18⅛ in. Tate Gallery, London. [Plate 25]

William TOWNSEND

Born 1909 in London. Studied at the Slade School. First one-man exhibition in London in 1932. Associated with the Euston Road School. Served in World War II. Taught at Camberwell School of Art and at the Slade School.

Hop Alleys. 1951–2. Oil, 30×20 in. Tate Gallery, London. [Plate 54]

Leon UNDERWOOD

Born 1890 in London. Studied at the Royal College of Art and the Slade School; also abroad. Served in Camouflage Sections in both World Wars. First one-man exhibition in London in 1923. Travelled widely in Iceland, Canada, U.S.A., Mexico, West Africa and elsewhere. Has written books on African sculpture and other subjects.

Torso: The June of Youth. 1937. Bronze, 24 in. high. Tate Gallery, London. [Plate 36]

Keith VAUGHAN

Born 1912 in Selsey Bill, Sussex. Self-taught. First one-man exhibition in London in 1942. Taught at the Central School of Arts and Crafts. Has travelled widely since World War II.

Nude against a Rock. 1957–58. Oil on board, 22×24 in. Coll. R. N. Kershaw, Esq., Wargrave. [Plate 150]
The Village. 1953. Oil, 29¾×10 in. Coll. The Arts Council of Great Britain. [Plate 151]

Edward WADSWORTH

Born 1889 in Cleckheaton, Yorkshire. Studied at the Knirr School, Munich, at the Bradford School of Art and at the Slade School. Served in World War I in the Eastern Mediterranean, and was later engaged on the dazzle camouflage of ships. First one-man exhibition in London in 1923. A lecture he delivered on "The Aesthetic Aspect of Civil Engineering" was published in 1945 in the Pro-

ceedings of the Institute of Civil Engineers. Died 1949. A retrospective exhibition held at the Tate Gallery in 1951.

Lit.: *Edward Wadsworth*, with contributions by Waldemar George, Michael Sevier and Ossip Zadkine (Sélection: Chronique de la vie artistique No. 13), Paris, 1933.

Marine. 1928. Tempera, 24½×34½ in. City Art Gallery, Leeds. [Plate 101]

Ethel WALKER

Born 1861 in Edinburgh. Studied at the Putney School of Art, at the Westminster and Slade Schools, and with Sickert. First one-man exhibition in London in 1936. Died 1951. Retrospective exhibition with Gwen John and Frances Hodgkins held at the Tate Gallery in 1952.

Vanessa. 1937. Oil, 24×30 in. Tate Gallery, London. [Plate 13]

Christopher WOOD

Born 1901 in Knowsley, near Liverpool. Studied briefly at the Académie Julian, Paris. Travelled widely in Europe and North Africa. First one-man exhibition in London in 1927, Cocteau writing the foreword to the catalogue. In 1923 met Picasso, who encouraged him and persuaded Diaghilev to invite Wood to design costumes and décor for "Romeo and Juliet", a ballet that was not performed. Owed encouragement, too, to Ben Nicholson. Killed by a train on Salisbury station, 1930. A memorial exhibition held in London in 1931 and retrospective exhibitions in 1938 and 1959.

Lit.: *Christopher Wood*, *1901–1930*, which contains an account of his life and work by Eric Newton, and list of works, 1938.

The Yellow Man. 1930. Oil, 20×24 in. Coll. Brinsley Ford, Esq., London. [Plate 97. Blocks kindly lent by the Redfern Gallery, London.]
The Yellow Horse. 1930. Oil, 20×24 in. Coll. Mrs. Lucy Carrington Wertheim, Brighton. [Plate 98]

Jack Butler YEATS

Born 1871 in London, son of John Butler Yeats, the painter, and brother of William Butler Yeats, the poet. Studied at the Westminster School of Art under Frederick Brown. Began to paint in oils in about 1897 and regularly from 1905. Illustrator and writer. Governor and Guardian of the National Gallery of Ireland. Retrospective exhibitions held at the National Gallery, London, in 1942, in Dublin in 1945, at Temple Newsam, Leeds, and the Tate Gallery in 1948. Although born and trained in England, Yeats was quintessentially an Irish painter and it was in Ireland that he passed the greater part of his life and from Ireland that he drew his subjects. Died 1957.

The Two Travellers. 1942. Oil, 9¼×14 in. Tate Gallery, London. [Plate 10]